THE DESIRE MAP

COURSE WORKBOOK

Return to your heart.
Choose your feelings.
Create your life with intention.

THE ONLINE COURSE + MANUAL FOR LIVING

COMMUNE

Danielle LAPORTE

OneCommune.com   **DanielleLaPorte.com**

Copyright © 2019 Danielle LaPorte, Inc.
#234 - 2055 Commercial Drive, Vancouver BC V5N 0C7 Canada
All rights reserved. Light excerpts are cool—with clear and obvious credit, please.
ISBN: 978-1-949709-52-0

THE DESIRE MAP UNIVERSE

Customer Service

desiremap@onecommune.com is standing by to answer your questions and hear your suggestions.

Group Purchases + Discounts

desiremap@onecommune.com will set you up with special pricing so you can gather your friends or workmates to start a Desire Map Course Club. We will also consider special pricing for cause-related organizations.

Danielle LaPorte Online

DANIELLELAPORTE.COM
weekly sermons about what I find in the cosmos—mostly, love.

@daniellelaporte
#Truthbombs, change agency, and being in touch.

@daniellelaporte
plentiful Pinterest beauty.

THEDESIREMAP.COM
find workshops, facilitators, coaches, and guidance.

@desiremap
weekly Desire Mapping inspiration.

Commune Online

ONECOMMUNE.COM
courses for personal and societal wellness.

@onecommune

cmn.to/desiremap
online support community.

Sharing is Caring

Hashtag it up so we can find you and return the love!

#desiremap #daniellelaporte #onecommune
+ @daniellelaporte @desiremap @onecommune

CONTENTS

THE DESIRE MAP UNIVERSE — 3

THANK YOU FOR BEING HERE — 7

BEGIN — 8

THE DESIRE MAP AT A GLANCE — 9

PART 1: DISCOVERING Your Core Desired Feelings

Soul Limber — 12
Gratitude — 14
What's Not Working — 18
Past + Present Feelings — 22
Desired Feelings: How I Want To Feel — 26
Inner Selves — 30
Broken Self + Whole Self — 32
Make Your First Picks — 34
Word Exploration — 35
Declare Your Core Desired Feelings — 37
Essential Qualities — 40
Expressions + Loves — 42
Breathe — 43

SUPPORT TOOLS

Core Desired Feeling Themes — 46
Positive, Pleasurable Feelings — 48
Negative, Unpleasant Feelings — 50

PART 2: CLARIFYING with Your Core Desired Feelings

Ideals + Favourites: Warm Up — 54
Inner World: Attitudes — 55
Inner World: Encouragement — 56
Outer World: Do/Experience + Have/Give — 57
Outer World: Stop Doing — 60

PART 3: PLANNING with Your Core Desired Feelings

Dream Analysis — 64
Goal Vetting Before Goal Setting — 66
Intention + Goal Setting — 68
Brutal Facts + Fears — 69

PART 4: LIVING Your Core Desired Feelings
THE DESIRE MAP MANUAL FOR LIVING

KEY PRACTICES
The Heart-Centering Practice 76
Create a Core Desired Feelings Blessing 80
Word Blessing Practice 81
Future Present 82
The Desire Map Manifesting Practice 84

GRATITUDE + FAITH PRACTICES
Even Deeper Gratitude 90
Building on Gratitude 91
Public Gratitude 92
Ratios of Gratitude 93
"What I Trust" List 94

REFRAMING PRACTICES
Align Your Thoughts 98
Present with the Negative 99
Feeling Anticipation 100
Forward Focus 101

DEEPER LIVING PRACTICES
How Will You Give of Yourself 104
Helpful People + Resources 105
Qualities + Expressions Reflection 106
Stay in Love with Your Core Desired Feelings 107
Inner Child Check In 108
Superhero Check In 108
Future Self Check In 108

HUGS + A REMINDER 111

THANK YOU FOR BEING HERE

Hello Love,

If you're reading this, you're part of THE DESIRE MAP COURSE—which means that you're in this for love . . . and clarity . . . and to be of service.

We of Team D, and our beloved friends at Commune, are so happy that you've shown up. We're all so deeply committed to personal and societal wellness, and this course, these pages, are one small way that we're trying to move the collective toward consciousness and joy—healing.

Like Rumi said, "There are a hundred ways to kneel and kiss the ground." There are so many roads and programs to freedom and fulfillment. This isn't the only path, but it's one that's built on the genius of the heart and it's helped a lot of people source and share their authentic power. So . . . do this. Be in it. Feel your way.

All heart,

BEGIN

A PRAYER FOR REFLECTION

I bring honour to my radiant heart,
courage to my deep questions,
respect to my true nature,
compassion to the collective.

May Spirit energize every step we
take toward love, truth, joy.

Thank you for the gifts of this
unfolding wisdom and beauty.

THE DESIRE MAP AT A GLANCE

THE LIFE AREAS

LIVELIHOOD + LIFESTYLE
Career. Work. Money. Home.
Things. Fashion. Travel.

BODY + WELLNESS
Fitness. Food. Rest + Relaxation. Healing.
Mental health. Sex + Sensuality.

CREATIVITY + LEARNING
Culture. Creative expression.
Education. Interests. Hobbies.

RELATIONSHIPS + SOCIETY
Romance. Partnership. Friendship.
Family. Children. Community. Causes.

ESSENCE + SPIRITUALITY
Soul. Inner self. Faith. Devotional practices.

THE PROCESS

Part 1:
DISCOVERING Your Core Desired Feelings

Part 2:
CLARIFYING with Your Core Desired Feelings

Part 3:
PLANNING with Your Core Desired Feelings

Part 4:
LIVING Your Core Desired Feelings
THE DESIRE MAP MANUAL FOR LIVING

PART 1:

DISCOVERING
YOUR CORE DESIRED FEELINGS

SOUL LIMBER

Our imagination shows us how we perceive reality.

> **Guidance**
>
> We're circling your desires and feelings before we dive straight into them. Soul Limber is meant to get you out of your head and more into your heart space. Less logic, more . . . liminal. Answer with the first thoughts that come to mind.

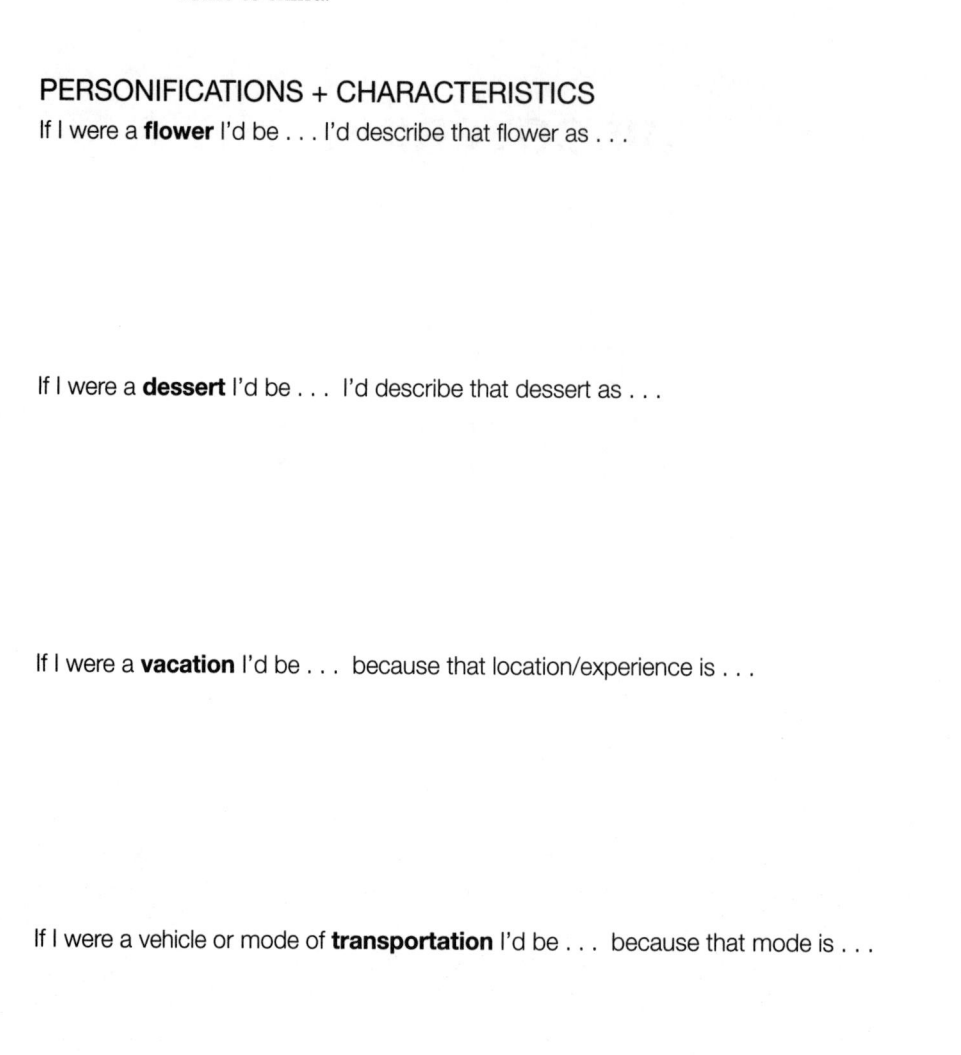

PERSONIFICATIONS + CHARACTERISTICS

If I were a **flower** I'd be . . . I'd describe that flower as . . .

If I were a **dessert** I'd be . . . I'd describe that dessert as . . .

If I were a **vacation** I'd be . . . because that location/experience is . . .

If I were a vehicle or mode of **transportation** I'd be . . . because that mode is . . .

CRAVINGS + VULNERABILITY

Other than time or money, what I **want more** of is . . .

I've felt **vulnerable** when . . .

I deal with **loneliness** by . . .

I'm **envious** of . . .

I'm **scared** of . . .

I need to give myself **permission** to be . . .

VITALITY + RESILIENCY

What I do most **naturally** is . . .

I've felt **doubtful** when . . .

I know when I'm **happy** because . . .

I **get through** tough times . . .

I feel most **alive** when . . .

What gives me so much **joy** . . .

GRATITUDE

Appreciation is a form of wellness.

Guidance

Gratitude. I am grateful . . . because . . .

In each life area, talk about what you're grateful for. Ramble on. Make your gratitude lists as long as you want! The longer the better.

Specificity increases the sensation of appreciation.

This is important . . . while you're naming off your gratitude in each life area, next to each thing that you say that you're grateful for, you'll be asked to complete this statement: "I'm grateful for this BECAUSE . . ."

Here's why: Being specific about what you're thankful for increases the sensation of appreciation, and that gives you access to even more positive feelings. You're going deeper into the sensuality and meaningfulness of circumstances and people in your life.

HINT: Some of those positive feelings you identify may turn out to be your Core Desired Feelings.

Cues

I'M GRATEFUL . . . *I love it. Adore it. Thankful. Thrilled. Brings me: joy, ease, comfort, delight. Appreciation. Value. Cherish.*

BECAUSE . . . *(**how/why** this brings benefit, ease, or happiness to you.)*

Within my **LIVELIHOOD + LIFESTYLE**

I'm grateful . . .

I'm grateful because . . .
(**how/why** this brings benefit, ease, or happiness to me).

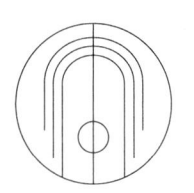

Within my **BODY + WELLNESS**

I'm grateful . . .

I'm grateful because . . .
(**how/why** this brings benefit, ease, or happiness to me).

Within my **CREATIVITY + LEARNING**

I'm grateful . . .

I'm grateful because . . .
(***how/why*** *this brings benefit, ease, or happiness to me*).

Within my **RELATIONSHIPS + SOCIETY**

I'm grateful . . .

I'm grateful because . . .
(***how/why*** *this brings benefit, ease, or happiness to me*).

Within my **ESSENCE + SPIRITUALITY**

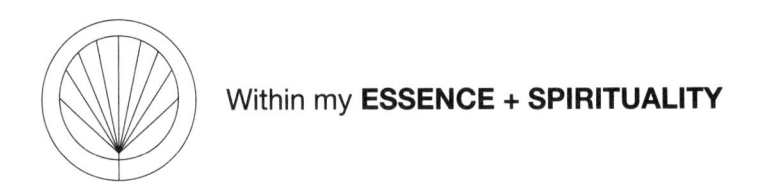

I'm grateful . . .

I'm grateful because . . .
(**how/why** this brings benefit, ease, or happiness to me).

Go Deeper.

My ideas for celebrating and/or creating even more of what I'm grateful for . . .

WHAT'S NOT WORKING

We need to get real about what's not working,
so we can make real changes.

Guidance

What's not working/needs to change ... because ...

We have to get real about the negatives in our lives so we can make a plan to transform them, or at least to *consciously* not pay attention to them (in which case, some of our so-called problems often tend to disappear).

Next to each thing that you note that isn't working, consider "WHY that issue is causing you negative stress or pain ..."

Approach this as an observer. You're a witness to the story. You are *noticing the type of things that aren't working.*

Healthy observations are these: what feels "off," out of alignment, painful, or incomplete. Unhealthy observations are lists of complaints, taking the position of self-victimization—of something that you feel is happening *to you*. Blaming. And that includes self-blame and criticism.

Stay in the witness mode, and try to simply notice what in your life is currently causing some suffering or frustration.

Don't go into fix-it mode yet. We're just observing.

Cues

WHAT'S NOT WORKING ... *I'm dissatisfied or frustrated. Disappointed, agitated, suffering.*

BECAUSE ... (**how/why** *this circumstance creates stress or pain*).

Within my **LIVELIHOOD + LIFESTYLE**

**What's not working/
needs to change . . .**

It's not working because . . .
(**how/why** this creates stress or pain)

Within my **BODY + WELLNESS**

**What's not working/
needs to change . . .**

It's not working because . . .
(**how/why** this creates stress or pain)

Within my **CREATIVITY + LEARNING**

**What's not working/
needs to change . . .**

It's not working because . . .
(***how/why*** *this creates stress or pain*)

Within my **RELATIONSHIPS + SOCIETY**

**What's not working/
needs to change . . .**

It's not working because . . .
(***how/why*** *this creates stress or pain*)

Within my ESSENCE + SPIRITUALITY

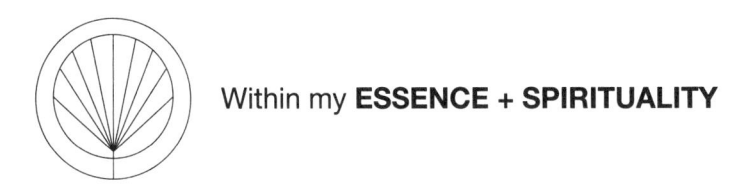

**What's not working/
needs to change . . .**

It's not working because . . .
(***how/why*** this creates stress or pain)

Go Deeper.

Now you can generate some ideas for changing—or accepting—what's not working. This may be the beginning of your STOP DOING LIST, which we'll get to down the road.

Some positive prompts to help think about what could change:

I could be at my best if . . .

It would make me feel so good if/to . . .

I feel supported when . . .

My ideal scenario is that . . .

PAST + PRESENT FEELINGS

Impactful and ongoing experiences create "feelings pathways/impressions" in our nervous system. We want to lay down pathways to more positive feelings.

PAST + PRESENT UNPLEASURABLE FEELINGS

Guidance

Recall some moments, events, happenings in your life where you felt not so great—IN THE PAST and PRESENTLY. Weighed down, stuck, at a loss. Of course there are spectrums of what "negative" feelings mean for each of us. That can range from getting a nasty comment on social media to your divorce, or from having your car towed to physical and emotional trauma—from slightly painful to serious impact. It's up to you what you want to identify as "negative." You don't need to drill to the depths of your psyche unless you're moved to go there. This can simply be about a few times when you just did not feel how you would have liked to in the particular situation.

As for the *present* negatives in your life, the simple and evocative question is: What are you tired of feeling? What feeling do you most certainly not want to be experiencing?

Refer to your **What's Not Working** list.

HINT: Your Core Desired Feelings are the opposite of unpleasurable feelings.

UM . . . NOT SO GREAT

PAST:
Unpleasant, negative occurrence/situation

I felt . . . I did not enjoy feeling . . .

PRESENT:
Unpleasant, negative occurrence/situation

I feel . . . I'm tired of feeling . . .

Go Deeper.

Positive feelings that contrast the negative feelings you listed above:

PAST + PRESENT PLEASURABLE FEELINGS

Guidance

Recall some moments, events, happenings in your life where you felt good—IN THE PAST and PRESENTLY. Joyful, alive, present, loving. What were you/are you doing where you felt/are feeling like your best self? Say . . . getting regular exercise, being in nature, learning about something you loved, spending time with your best friend. What memories and moments of your life helped/are helping you to experience joy and happiness?

Beside each instance, write down as specifically as possible, how you were/are feeling.

HIGHLY POSITIVE. LIKE, *SO* GOOD.

PAST:
Pleasurable, positive occurrence/situation

I felt . . . I enjoyed feeling . . .

PRESENT:
Pleasurable, positive occurrence/situation

I felt . . . I enjoy feeling . . .

Go Deeper

1. People you can connect with to say Thank You. Ways to continue the positive experiences . . .

2. Other similar feelings to the positive feelings you listed above would be . . .

DESIRED FEELINGS

Core Desired Feelings are qualities of the heart.

Let's root into this: Core Desired Feelings are your most preferred states of being. They are life-affirming, positive, expansive feelings. They are the various expressions of love and vitality. Core Desired Feelings are qualities of the heart, they pull you in the direction of your Highest Self, into gratitude, compassion, inclusivity, and generosity—your joy and peace in many forms.

Your Core Desired Feelings are your preferred states of being—the way you want to feel most of the time and most deeply.

Guidance

How do you want to feel in each of these areas of your life? Have a riff. Stream of consciousness is the way to go here. Ramble, jam, repeat yourself. Don't be concerned with duplicating words in different areas.

A desired feeling doesn't have to be summed up in just one single word. For example, "turned on" works. So does "at one with nature" or "passionately engaged."

Anything goes. Get abstract or specific. Do you want to feel spicy or red or electric? Do you want to feel ten different ways of confident? Then just write it down. Close your eyes and tune in. Let your wanted feelings flow freely. Do not censor yourself. Go deep, keep it light.

Let it flow, but you don't have to push yourself to come up with a huge number of words for the sake of variety. If you have only a few words in each section, then you might already be close to the heart of your matter.

Cues

Check out the SUPPORT TOOLS at the end of Part 1 (page 46) of the of the workbook: Core Desired Feelings Themes; Positive, Pleasurable Feelings; and Negative, Unpleasant Feelings.

HOW I WANT TO FEEL

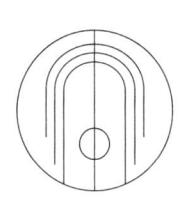

Within my **LIVELIHOOD + LIFESTYLE,** I want to feel . . .

Within my **BODY + WELLNESS,** I want to feel . . .

Within my **CREATIVITY + LEARNING,** I want to feel . . .

Within my **RELATIONSHIPS + SOCIETY,** I want to feel . . .

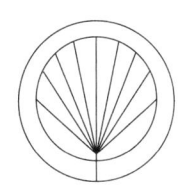

Within my **ESSENCE + SPIRITUALITY,** I want to feel . . .

INNER SELVES

See your feelings through your different inner selves—your tenderness, your strength, your trust.

> **Guidance**
>
> **Your Inner Child:** Imagine your childhood self, any age that comes to mind. Your Inner Child is that deeply sensitive part of you that deserves full attention, protection, and unconditional love. The part of you that usually thrives with gentleness and play.

Ask your **Inner Child how they NEED to feel in every LIFE AREA**. Their answers are likely simple and pure. Add those feelings to your lists.

> **Your Inner Superhero:** Every day is your best day ever. You have superpowers and are undefeatable. You are full of confidence and make no hesitations. You assume victory.

Ask your **Inner Superhero how they INTEND to feel** in every LIFE AREA. Add those feelings to your lists.

> **Your Future Self:** You don't need to see the specifics, but let's say in three to ten years from now, you're doing something incredible with your life. You're deeply well, you're where you belong with people who feel like home, you're full of Love.

Ask your **Future Self how they are ALREADY FEELING** in every LIFE AREA. You're getting their perspective from the future that has unfolded. Time travel FTW!

BROKEN SELF + WHOLE SELF

What you build on your self-value will be built to last.

Guidance

This is a big ask, but let's leap to it. **Assume that you are already whole and worthy. You're complete. You're divine. You're in.** Embrace that Universal Truth and let's work with self love and trust as our guidance system.

There's the type of desire that flows from **faith and self-valuing.** It's a desire that's building on its worthiness and sense of the possible. It's a desire that wants to go DEEPER and FULLER. *That's* the energy that we want to bring to our Core Desired Feelings. That desire flows from your heart center.

The opposite of that healthy desire is ego-based wanting. We want something that will fix our perceived brokenness. We want something to fill our emptiness. We think something outside of ourselves will complete us.

Try on both perspectives—brokenness and wholeness—and see if either viewpoint changes what you actually want. It may not. Maybe what you're desiring is being governed by your lack mentality, *as well as* your inner abundance—both can be at play. Perhaps if you're in a place of fulfillment and you really don't have any cravings for more. Or you could be as determined as ever to create what you're desiring. Let's see . . .

1. TEMPORARILY GO TO THIS ZONE: BROKEN.

This is only an exercise, you're not sending a direct signal to the Universe. Okay? Okay.

Imagine that you feel: broken, defective, in need of fixing. You think you're behind in life. You wonder if you'll ever catch up, you question if your dreams are even possible. Doubt is floating around. It's hard to imagine being fulfilled.

Now! What do you think you need to feel to heal your brokenness? What do you crave to feel?

2. NOW GO HERE: WHOLE.

Take in this truth, let it fill every cell: **you are complete, safe, loved, and loving.** You are a Divine Being and Life rejoices in fulfilling your desires—you and life are in a dynamic collaboration. You're perfect in Creation's eyes. All Love and wisdom dwell within in. You radiate beauty and joy. You live in an abundant, trusting state of flow. Repeat: **you are complete, safe, loved, loving, and Life is holding you.**

Now! From that place of wholeness, you may not desire anything at all. Your cravings seem to have melted away. You ACCEPT YOUR WHOLENESS! You can flow with Life. If that's what you're sensing and perceiving, then the question is: **What *else* do you feel in that state of wholeness? What other feelings would be a celebration of your wholeness?**

MAKE YOUR FIRST PICKS

Focus increases your potency.

Guidance

Narrow down to 10 to 12 potential Core Desired Feelings. Refer to your DESIRED FEELINGS exercise and your INNER SELVES exercise and **circle the feeling words that resonate** with you the most. You can always put a word back in the mix if you pass it over in this first round. Trust your instincts and preferences. The truth wants to surface and you are creating space for it to rise up.

Patterns. You want to find the redundancies and overlaps between various words so that you can knock some words off your list and zero in on the most empowering selections for yourself.

Be aware of grand words. Be especially vigilant to look beneath big, sweeping concepts and words such as "successful" or "confident."

Do you have a sense of pressure or proving yourself around a certain word?

WORD EXPLORATION

Every word is a universe.

Guidance

Word Exploration. Dictionary and thesaurus time! Get inside the words. **Look up the definitions and synonyms** of the words you've circled so far. Check out their origins, etymology, languages, uses. When you read the actual definitions, do the words take on a new or more **powerful meaning?** Do they feel more **masculine or feminine?** What nuances are in the words that you **relate** to? Do the origins of certain words inspire or repel you? Do you have a positive or negative **history** with that word?

Personal associations. Official word definitions won't always match up with contemporary understanding or your personal vibe. You may find that some words that you really love have sort of old-school moralistic definitions that turn you off. Ultimately, you have to define each word for yourself; it only needs to fit into your psyche, not Webster's history. You can either let the dictionary definition play into your word choices and impressions of the words, or choose to go with your own intuitive connotations and even revise the dictionary definitions based on your own experiences.

You can get way out of the box if you want. We've heard of some amazing CDFs over the years. Anything goes: Badass. Water. Kind of a Big Deal. Lioness. Neon. Firecracker. Spicy. Supernova. Symphonic. Caliente. Mother. Ocean.

Grow. Add new words if you want to. Do you see new feelings in the thesaurus or definitions that you gravitate toward? Write those down as well.

Narrow down to 7 or so potential Core Desired Feelings: Focusing on core feelings is a critical part of this practice. Core desires = unlimited power. If you have a lot of desired feelings on your final list, it's more difficult to focus. Eventually, we'll get this down to 4 or 5 words—a short list that you can easily remember.

MY *POTENTIAL* CORE DESIRED FEELINGS . . .

And the finalists are . . .
Collect all of your short-listed words here.

DECLARE YOUR CORE DESIRED FEELINGS

Live from the heart.

As Carl Jung put it, "Only the dreamer knows the dream." You know what your Core Desired Feelings are. The meaning of each word or phrase is for you to own and interpret. It does not have to fit a formula. It doesn't have to be workable or realistic for anyone else—not even your best friend or therapist. Feel your feelings. Aim.

Guidance

Of your short-listed feeling words, which words make you feel:

Expansive and energized?

Grounded and peaceful?

Home and blessed?

Reminder, the definition of a Core Desired Feeling: Your Core Desired Feelings are how you want to feel most of the time—your most preferred states of being. They're life-affirming feelings—positive and expansive. They're qualities of the heart—expressions of love and vitality. Your Core Desired Feelings move you toward your Highest Self—to joy, inclusivity, and generosity.

Authenticity: Apply this question to the words you're most attracted to:

What is [insert potential Core Desired Feeling] *really* **about for me?** For example, maybe "confidence" is really about feeling empowered, or elegant, or maybe it's about respect. Maybe "success" is really about freedom, or love, or being collaborative. Maybe "beautiful" is really about connection or radiance . . .

If you want to keep more than five feelings, go right ahead. If seven is your lucky number, then choose seven words for luck. Fewer words might help you get better results because fewer is much easier to recall, but doing this in a way that works for you is what's most important.

Make your selections! Choose your four or five Core Desired Feelings—and shine. This is the moment. I'm thinking of you right now, sending love, and whispering into your ear: Core . . . Desired . . . Feelings.

Write your Core Desired Feelings on the following page, and if you like, include the definition or synonyms of each word and/or what that word means to you.

MY CORE DESIRED FEELINGS

Go Deeper.

Fun with CDFs!

Compose an **affirmative phrase** (in the present) or **action statement** with your Core Desired Feelings.

Examples:

Purpose. Ease. Adventure. = *I'm creating an **adventurous** life of **purpose**, and I live in **ease**.*

Connection. Radiant. Joyful. Vitality. = *I experience **joyful connection** with everyone and everything around me. My **vitality** fuels my **radiance**.*

Make an **acronym** for memory recall: Freedom. Receptive. Elegance. Ease. = F.R.E.E.

Put your CDFs in an **order** that gives them a kind of "magical sequence," one leads to the other. *Creativity Flowing Prosperity* or *Fulfilling Joy Connection.*

ESSENTIAL QUALITIES

If your Core Desired Feeling was a character in your play . . .

> ## Guidance
>
> Let's bring more colour and texture to each of your CDFs. The more dimensional and vibrant each word is, the easier it will be to access as a feeling. You want to KNOW and call on that Core Desired Feeling like you would turn to a beloved friend.

What are the ESSENTIAL QUALITIES of each of your Core Desired Feelings?

Essential Qualities are the characteristics or the traits of that feeling—how it expresses itself in the world. Naming just a few qualities can help you root into your CDF.

Examples:

Grounded = gets 8 hours of sleep. Doesn't overschedule. Eats organic. Makes decisions with ease. Is deliberate. Surrounds oneself with nourishing people. Loves plants. Hikes. Simplifies.

Vitality = fresh water. Comedy shows. Prana breathing. New bright pillows. Sunday service. Functional medicine. Monthly support group. SMILES, hugs, leans in.

Or! You can write your CDF's characteristics in a poetic and descriptive way:

Examples:

Connection . . . is present and open. She's a good friend. He looks for what's lovable in everyone. Connection's favourite word is "resonance." She shares intimately and deeply—when she feels there is harmony and receptivity. Connection keeps in touch, plans celebrations, makes eye contact. Connection references its body for signals of the truth. He prays. She forms community. Connection plays. Connection thrives with some stillness and silence.

Sacred Feminine . . . is receptive and nourishing. Sacred Feminine receives like a trusting daughter and a graceful Queen. She loves to give her love. She/he is gentle. She is fierce and discerning. She gets to the heart of the matter. Sacred Feminine protects her loved ones. She dances a lot, eats flowers, upholds human dignity. She celebrates her pleasure. She stays close to nature, listens deeply, breathes through the heart. Sacred Feminine is a possibility thinker, feeling deeply, acting with loving kindness.

Ease . . . is the cousin of simplicity. Ease can let it go. Ease chooses the easiest way without compromising its standards. She can be very forgiving. He trusts that life is guiding him. Ease doesn't give into time pressure—she can be brisk or she can languish, it depends on what feels easy in the moment. Ease is about being close to LIFE, and removing obstacles to that vitality.

Core Desired Feeling	Essential Qualities

EXPRESSIONS + LOVES

What brings your Core Desired Feeling to life?

> ## Guidance
> Your Core Desired Feeling has . . . desires and feelings. Let it express itself.

	Core Desired Feeling _____	Core Desired Feeling _____	Core Desired Feeling _____	Core Desired Feeling _____	Core Desired Feeling _____
Loves to . . .					
Adores . . .					
Feels joy when . . .					
Remembers . . .					
Wears . . .					
Listens to . . .					
Eats . . .					
Moves . . .					
Celebrates . . .					
Cherishes . . .					
Protects . . .					
Gives to . . .					
Delights in . . .					

BREATHE

You've honed in on your Core Desired Feelings. Finally . . . Chills! Brilliant. **Beautiful.** Some people go their entire lives on autopilot of do-get-do-get, and you've just cracked a code to deeper living. Now . . . breathe.

LET IT STEW. Don't tattoo your Core Desired Feelings anywhere—yet (it's been done. As an author I should act impartial about tattoos related to my work. But . . . so cool). Move on to the next phase of Desire Mapping, but know that this can be a trial run. Feelings are fluid and this practice should be as well. You can feel out your words for a few weeks and go back and tweak them for fit. This is an art, not a science.

COMPARE NOTES, BUT DON'T COMPARE YOURSELF. Sharing your discoveries with a friend is a great thing to do. Just be sure to avoid the trap of hearing someone else's CDFs and then changing your own because you've now decided they are less awesome, cool, or noble than the other person's.

BE OPEN TO CHANGE. Will your Core Desired Feelings change over time? Probably. But maybe not. I held on to my very first set of CDFs for a few years. Now I refresh them whenever I feel like it, but on the whole, I tend to work with the same CDFs for at least a year. Some keep getting recycled like a cherished ring that you put away for a few months, but always bring it back into circulation.

The important thing is to stay curious and alive with your Core Desired Feelings. If they don't keep their glow, you can't use them as a guidance system.

REST. Take a hot bath. Walk around the block. Do some kitchen disco. Have a happy cry, call a friend. Take a break—for a few hours or a couple of days. I'll be here when you get back. And please, keep coming back.

COMMUNING

There's a legion of kind souls who are Desire Mapping, and Team D + Commune are a fount of loving guidance.

Head to **cmn.to/desiremap**—to access the supportive, kindness-based Desire Map Community. There are Desire Map Facilitators and Coaches to cheer you on, and so many of us who are committed to heart-centered living.

You can find all of us on Instagram @desiremap @daniellelaporte and on Facebook at DesireMap.com/Facebook

SUPPORT TOOLS

CORE DESIRED FEELING THEMES

Thanks to thousands of Desire Mappers in many countries, we've noticed a pattern in Core Desired Feelings—fundamental feelings that many of us long for and identify with at some point in our lives. Here are the twelve key themes that have emerged:

BEAUTY + SENSUALITY   LOVE + CONNECTION
FREEDOM + POWER   PEACE + FLOW
JOY + VITALITY   RADIANCE + SPIRIT

BEAUTY + SENSUALITY

Alluring, Balance, Beatific, Dance, Desire, Ecstasy, Embodied, Enchanted, Enthralled, Erotic, Eros, Fervor, Gorgeous, Graceful, Harmony, Indulgence, Intimate, Irresistible, Lush, Luxury, Orgasmic, Passion, Passionate, Pleasure, Pride, Sacred Feminine, Sacred Masculine, Savouring, Sensual, Sensuous, Sexy, Succulent, Wild, Whole, Yoga

FREEDOM + POWER

Adventurous, Assured, Audacious, Autonomous, Badass, Birth, Bold, Boundless, Brave, Brave Heart, Bravery, Brilliance, Brilliant, Charged, Clear, Confident, Courageous, Curious, Daring, Dominion, Dynamic, Ease, Effectual, Electric, Elevated, Emboldened, Empowered, Empowering, Epic, Expansion, Expansive, Exploring, Fierce, Generosity, Generous, Gumption, Gutsy, Heroic, Holistic, Hope, Hopeful, In Charge, Independence, Independent, Influencing, Influential, Innovative, Integrity, King/Queen, Liberated, Magnificent, Majestic, Mastery, Maverick, Mighty, Open, Openhearted, Outspoken, Phenomenal, Potent, Power, Powerful, Regal, Release, Resilience, Resilient, Sovereign, Sovereignty, Spacious, Strength, Strong, Substance, Superman, Tenacious, Trailblazer, Unleashed, Vocal, Voice, Voicing, Warrior, Wild, Wisdom, Wise, Wonder Woman, Zeal

JOY + VITALITY

Alive, Artful, Beautiful, Beauty, Bliss, Blissed, Blissful, Bright, Brilliance, Brilliant, Buoyant, Celebration, Cheerful, Colourful, Contributing, Creating, Creative, Curious, Deeply Well, Delight, Delightful, Delighting, Driven, Dynamic, Dynamism, Eager, Ebullient, Effervescent, Elation, Electric, Encouraged, Energetic, Enjoyment, Euphoria, Euphoric, Excited, Excitement, Exciting, Expressive, Extraordinary, Exuberance, Fecund, Felicity, Fertile, Fertility, Festive, Flourish, Focused, Fresh, Fruitful, Fun, Giddy, Given, Giving, Glee, Gleeful, Happiness, Happy, Health, High, Hope, Hopeful, Illumined, Imaginative, Invigorated, Jazzed, Joy, Joyful, Joyous, Jubilant, Keen, Light, Lightness, Lit Up, Lively, Luminary, Luminous, Magic, Manifesting, New, Nourished, Offering, Optimism, Optimistic, Playful, Poetic, Prolific, Rapture, Rested, Restorative, Restored, Shakti, Spark, Stimulated, Stoked, Sunrise, Sunshine, Thrill, Thriving, Unleashed, Upbeat, Verve, Verdant, Vibrancy, Vibrant, Visionary, Vital, Vivacious, Vivacity, Vivid, Well, Wellness, Wild, Wisdom, Wise, Young at Heart, Youthful

LOVE + CONNECTION

Abundance, Abundant, Adoring, Adoration, Affection, Altruistic, Authentic, Beauty, Being, Beingness, Belonging, Beloved, Brotherhood, Camaraderie, Care, Caring, Caritas, Celebrated, Cherish, Chosen, Choosing, Close, Collaborative, Commitment, Committed, Communion, Community, Compassion, Compassionate, Complete, Dance, Deserving, Devotion, Devoted, Earnest, Embrace, Embracing, Enamoured, Encourage, Family, Father, Fathering, Friendship, Gaia, Generous, Generosity, Gentle, Genuine, Giving, Grace, Harmony, Heartened, Held, Humanity, In Circle, Intentional, Intimacy, Joy, Kin, Kind, Kindness, Kindred, Lovable, Love, Lover, Lovely, Loving, Meeting, Met, More Than Enough, Mother, Mothering, Natural, Nourishment, Nurtured, Nurturing, One, Partnering, Partnership, Peace, Precious, Presence, Present, Receptive, Recognition, Remarkable, Resilient, Respect, Seen, Sharing, Sisterhood, Sweet, Tender, Thoughtful, Together, Treasure, Trust, Unconditional, Understood, Union, Unification, Unified, Unifying, Unity, Valuable, Warmth, Whole, Wholehearted

PEACE + FLOW

Acceptance, Accepting, Accommodating, Agreeable, Aligned, Allowing, Anchored, At Home, Attuned, Authentic, Balanced, Beingness, Bliss, Blissful, Breezy, Centered, Certain, Comfort, Comfortable, Comforting, Complete, Cool, Cozy, Deep, Earthy, Ease, Easeful, Effortless, Embodied, Engaged, Essential, Evolution, Flexible, Fluid, Free, Generosity, Generous, Grace, Graceful, Gracious, Grounded, Harmony, Immersed, Inclusive, Intentional, In My Element, In Sync, In the Zone, In Tune, Lithe, Masterful, Momentum, Natural, On Purpose, Presence, Present, Protected, Protection, Purposeful, Ready, Relaxed, Renewal, Renewed, Resonance, Resonating, Rest, Restorative, Restored, Rooted, Safe, Secure, Soul, Synchronous, Synergy, Tuned-in, Water, Zen

RADIANCE + SPIRIT

Ablaze, Allied, Amazement, Angels, Anointed, Ardent, Ascension, Awakened, Awe, Awesome, Beauty, Beloved, Blazing, Blessed, Bright, Brilliant, Celestial, Chosen, Communion, Conscious, Contemplative, Cosmic, Dazzling, Deep, Devotion, Divine, Divine Feminine, Divine Masculine, Divinely Favoured, Emanating, Enlightened, Essence, Ethereal, Expansive, Faith, Fire, Glowing, God, Goddess, Gold, Gratitude, Guided, Heart, Heart-centered, Heartful, High Spirits, Holy, Hopeful, Illuminated, Infinite, Lit Up, Lovely, Lucid, Luminous, Mindful, Miracle, Nirvana, Prayerful, Pure, Radiance, Radiant, Rainbow, Reflection, Reverence, Sacred, Sacred Feminine, Sacred Masculine, Satisfied, Shimmering, Simplicity, Spark, Sparkle, Spirit, Transcendence, Transcendent, Truth, Truthful, Turned On, Uplifted, Vast, Voice, Wakeful

Some cool and quirky CDFs we've heard over the years: Agora, Aloha, Atmospheric, Caliente, Creatrix, Crème de la Crème, Empress, Feral, Firecracker, Halcyon, High Voltage, Hygge, Kali, Kind of a Big Deal, Lambent, Lioness-hearted, Masterpeace, Meraki, Mermaid, Mother, Neon, Ocean, One of a Kind, Quite at Home, Rollin', Sea, Soul Sassy, Spicy, Sunshine, Supernova, Symphonic, Wanderlust, Warrior, Water, Waves, Welcome, Wicked, Yellow

POSITIVE, PLEASURABLE FEELINGS

- A -

Ablaze, Abundance, Abundant, Acceptance, Accepted, Accepting, Accommodating, Accomplished, Acknowledged, Adaptable, Admiration, Adoration, Adoring, Advancing, Adventure, Affection, Affectionate, Affluent, Agile, Agreeable, Alchemical, Aligned, Alive, Allied, Allowed, Allowing, Alluring, Altruistic, Amazement, Amazing, Ambitious, Ambrosial, Amour, Anchored, Angels, Animated, Anointed, Anticipation, Appreciated, Appreciation, Ardent, Ardor, Artful, Articulate, Artistic, Ascension, Assertive, Assured, Astounding, Attentive, Attractive, Attuned, Audacious, Auspicious, Authentic, Awake, Aware, Awe, Awesome

- B -

Badass, Balance, Balanced, Beatific, Beautiful, Beauty, Being, Beingness, Belonging, Beloved, Benevolent, Birth, Blazing, Blessed, Blessing, Bliss, Blissed Out, Blissful, Blooming, Blossoming, Bold, Boundless, Bountiful, Brave, Brave Heart, Bravery, Breakthrough, Breezy, Bright, Brilliance, Brilliant, Brimming, Brother/Sisterhood, Buoyant, Buzzing

- C -

Caliente, Calm, Calming, Camaraderie, Capable, Care, Cared For, Carefree, Caring, Caritas, Catalyst, Celebrated, Celebration, Celebratory, Celestial, Centered, Certain, Certitude, Charmed, Cheer, Cheerful, Cherished, Cherishing, Childlike, Chosen, Clarity, Classy, Clean, Clear, Close, Cocooned, Cocreator, Collaborative, Colourful, Comfort, Comfortable, Comforting, Commitment, Committed, Communing, Communion, Community, Compassion, Compassionate, Complete, Confidence, Confident, Connected, Connection, Consciousness, Content, Contentment, Continuous, Cool, Cosmic, Courage, Courageous, Cozy, Crafted, Creating, Creation, Creative, Creativity, Curious, Current

- D -

Dance, Daring, Dauntless, Dazzling, Decisive, Declare, Dedicated, Deep, Deeply Well, Deliberate, Delicious, Delight, Delighted, Delightful, Delighting, Depth, Deserving, Desire, Desired, Determination, Determined, Devoted, Devotion, Diligence, Disciplined, Discovery, Divine, Divinely Favoured, Driven, Dynamic, Dynamism

- E -

Eager, Earnest, Earth, Earthy, Ease, Easeful, Easy, Ebullient, Eccentric, Ecstasy, Ecstatic, Effective, Effervescent, Elated, Elation, Electric, Elegance, Elegant, Elemental, Elevated, Eloquent, Embodied, Emboldened, Embrace, Embracing, Emergent, Empowered, Empowering, Enamoured, Enchanted, Encouraged, Encouragement, Encouraging, Endless, Enduring, Energetic, Energized, Energy, Engaged, Enjoyment, Enlightened, Enlightening, Enraptured, Enriched, Enthralled, Enthusiasm, Enthusiastic, Enticing, Epic, Equanimity, Eros, Erotic, Essential, Ethereal, Euphoria, Euphoric, Ever-expanding, Evolution, Evolved, Excellence, Exceptional, Excited, Excitement, Exciting, Exhilarated, Exhilarating, Expansion, Expansive, Explorer, Exploring, Expressed, Expressive, Exquisite, Extraordinary, Exuberance

- F -

Fabulous, Faith, Faithful, Family, Fantastic, Fantastical, Fascinated, Fascinating, Fascination, Father, Fathering, Fearless, Fecund, Felicity, Fellowship, Feminine, Femininity, Fertile, Fervent, Fervor, Festive, Fierce, Firecracker, Fit, Flamboyant, Flexible, Flirtatious, Flourish, Flourishing, Flow, Flowing, Fluid, Flush, Focus, Focused, Forgiven, Forgiving, Fortunate, Fortune, Free, Free Spirited, Free-flowing, Freedom, Fresh, Friendliness, Friendly, Friendship, Fruitful, Fulfilled, Full, Fun, Fun Loving

- G -

Gaia, Gallant, Generative, Generosity, Generous, Gentle, Gentleness, Genuine, Giddy, Given, Giving, Glad, Glamorous, Glee, Gleeful, Glorious, Glory, Glowing, God, Goddess, Gold, Golden, Goodwill, Gorgeous, Grace, Graceful, Gracious, Grateful, Gratified, Gratitude, Grit, Groovy, Grounded, Growth, Guidance, Guided, Gumption, Gutsy

- H -

Happiness, Happy, Harmonious, Harmony, Heal, Healed, Healing, Healthy, Heard, Heart, Heart-centered, Heartened, Heartful, Heaven-sent, Held, Helpful, Heroic, High, High Spirits, Holistic, Holy, Home, Homey, Honest, Honor, Hope, Hopeful, Hot, Humanity, Humility, Hunger, Hygge

- I -

Ignited, Illuminated, Imaginative, Immersed, Impactful, Important, Impractical, In Awe, In Circle, In Communion, In Flow, In Love, In My Element, In My Full Essence, In Service to Others, In the Flow, In the Zone, In Tune, Incandescent, Included, Inclusive, Incomparable, Incredible, Independence, Indigo, Indomitable, Indulgence, Indulgent, Ineffable, Infamous, Infinite, Influencing, Influential, Innovating, Innovation, Innovative, Inquisitive, Insightful, Inspiration, Inspirational, Inspired, Inspiring, Instinctive, Integrity, Integrous, Intent, Intentional, Interdependent, Intimate, Intoxicating, Intrepid, Intrigued, Intriguing, Intuitive, Invigorated, Invincible, Invocation, Irrepressible, Irresistible

- J -

Jazzed, Joie de Vivre, Joy, Joy-filled, Joyful, Joyous, Joyride, Jubilant, Jubilation, Juiced Up, Juicy

- K -

Karmic, Keen, Kick-ass, Kind, Kindness, Kindred, King, Kinship, Knowing, Knowledgeable

- L -

Laughter, Lavish, Lean, Legacy making, Legitimacy, Letting Go, Liberated, Liberation, Life-giving, Light, Lighthearted, Lightness, Limitless, Lion(ess)-hearted, Lit, Lit Up, Lithe, Lively, Living On My Creative Edge, Loose, Lovable, Love, Loved, Lovely, Loverly, Loving, Loyal, Lucid, Lucky, Lucrative, Luminary, Luminous, Lupine, Lusciousness, Lush, Luxurious

- M -

Magic, Magical, Magnetic, Magnificent, Maitri, Maker, Making a Difference, Manifesting, Masculine, Masculinity, Masterful, Masterpiece, Mastery, Maverick, Meaning, Meeting, Mesmerizing, Mighty, Mindful, Mindfulness, Miracle, Miraculous, Mobile, Momentum, More Than Enough, Mother, Mothering, Motivated, Motivational, Mouthwatering, Moved, Moxie, Multidimensional, Mysterious, Mystical

- N -

Natural, Neon, New, Nimble, Nirvana, Noble, Nourish, Nourished, Novaturient, Nurtured, Nurturing

- O -

Ocean, Oceanic, Of Service, Offering, Olympic, On, On Fire, On Purpose, One, Oneness, Open, Open-minded, Openhearted, Openness, Optimistic, Opulence, Opulent, Order, Organic, Organized, Orgasmic, Original, Otherworldly, Outrageous, Outspoken, Overflowing, Overjoyed

- P -

Partnering, Partnership, Passion, Passion-driven, Passionate, Patient, Peace, Peaceful, Perfection, Perfectly Imperfect, Perseverance, Phenomenal, Philanthropic, Phoenix, Pioneer, Pizzazz, Playful, Pleased, Pleasure, Plenty, Pluck, Plucky, Plugged In, Poetic, Poetry, Positive, Potent, Power, Powerful, Practical, Precious, Prepared, Presence, Present, Pretty, Pride, Primal, Prime, Productive, Professional, Profound, Progressive, Prolific, Prosperous, Protected, Protection, Proud, Prowess, Pulsating, Pumped, Pure, Purpose, Purposeful

- Q -

Queen, Quenched, Quiet

- R -

Radiant, Radical, Rainbow, Rapport, Rapture, Rapturous, Ready, Real, Realized, Receptive, Recognition, Recognized, Refreshed, Regal, Regenerative, Relaxation, Relaxed, Relaxing, Released, Reliable, Relief, Relieved, Remarkable, Renewal, Renewed, Replenished, Repose, Reposed, Resilience, Resilient, Resolute, Resonance, Resonating, Respect, Respected, Resplendent, Rest, Rested, Restorative, Restored, Revealed, Reverence, Reverent, Rich, Riches, Righteous, Rock 'n' Roll, Rollin', Romance, Rooted, Rosy, Royal

- S -

Sacred, Sacred Feminine, Sacred Masculine, Safe, Satiated, Satisfied, Savour, Secure, Seductive, Seen, Self Kindness, Self Nurtured, Self-actualized, Self-care, Self-sufficient, Sensual, Sensuous, Serene, Serenity, Service, Sexual, Sexy, Shakti, Shimmering, Shine, Shining, Significant, Silly, Simplicity, Sisterhood, Smart, Soft, Softness, Solace, Solar, Solid, Solid Gold, Soothed, Sophisticated, Sophrosyne, Soul, Soul Centered, Soul Filled, Soul Satisfied, Soulful, Soulmate, Sound, Sourced, Sovereign, Space, Spacious,

Spark, Sparkle, Spectacular, Spicy, Spirit, Spirit Guided, Spirited, Spiritual, Spunky, Stable, Star, Steadfast, Steady, Steeped, Still, Stimulated, Stoked, Strength, Strong, Structured, Sublime, Substance, Successful, Succulent, Sultry, Sunrise, Sunshine, Super, Superb, Superdeluxe, Supernova, Supple, Supplied, Supported, Supportive, Supreme, Sure, Surreal, Surrender, Sweet, Symphonic, Synchronous, Synergy

- T -

Tadasana, Thanks, Temperance, Tenacious, Tenacity, Tender, Tethered, Thankful, Thoughtful, Thrilled, Thrilling, Thriving, Timeless, Together, Touched, Trailblazer, Tranquil, Tranquillity, Transcendence, Transcendent, Transformative, Transformed, Treasure, Treasured, Treasuring, Triumphant, True, Trust, Trustworthy, Truth, Truthful, Tuned-in, Turned On

- U -

Unconditional, Unconditional Love, Understanding, Understood, Unfolded, Unification, Unified, Unifying, Union, Unique, United, Unity, Unleashed, Unwrapped, Upbeat, Uplifted, Useful

- V -

Validated, Valor, Valuable, Valued, Vast, Versatile, Verve, Vibrancy, Vibrant, Victorious, Vigor, Visceral, Visible, Visionary, Vital, Vitality, Vivacious, Vivacity, Vivid, Vocal, Voice, Voicing, Voluptuous, Vulnerable

- W -

Wakeful, Wanderlust, Warm, Warmth, Warrior, Water, Wealthy, Welcome, Well, Well-being, Well-crafted, Whimsical, Whimsy, Whole, Wholehearted, Wholesome, Wild, Wild-hearted, Willing, Wisdom, Wise, Witty, Wonder, Wonder Woman, Wonderful, Worldly, Worthy

- Y -

Yoga, Young at Heart, Youthful

- Z -

Zeal, Zealous, Zen, Zoetic

NEGATIVE, UNPLEASURABLE FEELINGS

- A -

Abandoned, Addicted, Afraid, Aggravated, Aggressive, Alarmed, Alienated, Ambivalent, Angry, Annoyed, Anxious, Apprehensive, Ashamed, Awkward

- B -

Bereaved, Betrayed, Bitter, Blocked, Blue, Bored, Bothered, Broken, Burdened

- C -

Cautious, Cold, Complacent, Compulsive, Concerned, Conflicted, Confused, Contemptuous, Contributing, Contrite, Controlling, Cranky, Crestfallen, Critical, Cruel, Crushed

- D -

Defeated, Defensive, Defiant, Dejected, Depressed, Detached, Devastated, Devious, Disappointed, Disconnected, Discouraged, Disdainful, Disenchanted, Disengaged, Disgusted, Disillusioned, Disinterested, Dismayed, Dismissive, Distant, Distracted

- E -

Embarrassed, Empty, Enraged, Envious, Exhausted

- F -

Fatigued, Fearful, Flawed, Flustered, Foolish, Frightened, Frozen, Frustrated, Furious

- G -

Gloomy, Greedy, Grief-stricken, Grouchy, Grumpy, Guarded, Guilty

- H -

Heartbroken, Helpless, Hesitant, Hopeless, Horrified, Humiliated, Hurt

- I -

Ignorant, Impatient, Impertinent, Inadequate, Indifferent, Insecure, Irked, Irrational, Irritable, Irritated, Isolated

- J -

Jaded, Jealous, Judged, Judgmental

- K -

Killjoy

- L -

Lackluster, Lazy, Leery, Lethargic, Listless, Lonely, Lost

- M -

Mad, Malevolent, Manic, Manipulated, Manipulative, Mean, Meek, Melancholy, Melodramatic, Miserable, Misunderstood, Moody, Mopey, Morose

- N -

Nasty, Needy, Neglected, Neglectful, Nervous, Numb

- O -

Obligated, Obsessive, Offended, Outraged, Overpowered, Overstimulated, Overwhelmed, Overworked

- P -

Pained, Panicked, Paranoid, Passive, Peeved, Persecuted, Perturbed, Pessimistic, Petrified, Petty, Petulant, Powerless, Preoccupied, Pressured, Prickly

- Q -

Quarrelsome

- R -

Rattled, Reluctant, Remorseful, Repressed, Repulsed, Resentful, Restless, Rigid

- S -

Sad, Sarcastic, Scared, Scornful, Selfish, Serious, Shocked, Shy, Sick, Skeptical, Sorrowful, Spiteful, Startled, Stressed, Stubborn, Stuck, Suffocated, Suspicious

- T -

Temperamental, Tense, Terrified, Threatened, Timid, Tired, Tiresome, Torn, Trapped, Triggered, Troubled

- U -

Ugly, Unappreciated, Uncertain, Uncomfortable, Undecided, Uneasy, Ungrateful, Unhappy, Unheard, Unimpressed, Unnerved, Unruly, Unseen, Unsettled, Unsteady, Unsure, Uptight, Used, Useless

- V -

Vain, Vacant, Vexed, Victimized, Violent, Volatile

- W -

Wary, Wasted, Weak, Weary, Weepy, Whiny, Wired, Withdrawn, Woeful, Worn, Worthless, Wronged, Worried

- Y -

Yearning

PART 2:

CLARIFYING
WITH YOUR CORE DESIRED FEELINGS

IDEALS + FAVOURITES: WARM UP

Flow with your preferences.

> **Guidance**
>
> This might feel like a dating app questionnaire, but go with it. What we're doing here is pulling up favourite and fantasy experiences. And then you'll start matching your Core Desired Feelings with desired things to do/experience + have/give.

My currently ideal and/or favourite . . .

Way to spend my birthday . . .

Summer vacation . . .

Sunday . . .

Morning routine . . .

Way to spend alone time . . .

INNER WORLD: ATTITUDES

Every Desire Map step brings more inner attunement, which creates more meaningful outer attainment.

> ## Guidance
>
> Each Core Desired Feeling is an expression of our true self. When we focus on generating a particular feeling, we're animating an aspect of our truth.
>
> This can be a really profound introspection. Essentially, we're looking at how the attitude we're holding intensifies or dilutes our desired feelings. We need to choose perspectives that help our Core Desired Feelings to emerge.

FEELINGS inform THOUGHTS inform BEHAVIOUR. In this exercise we're **creating thoughts that support our feelings.** What's the "inner attitude" that will help you generate a particular feeling?

Example:

I feel Flow more when I'm thinking more optimistically. I feel Luminous more when I'm trusting in God. I feel Expansive more when I let go of my belief that I have to earn my keep . . .

_____ requires me to **be more . . .**
[insert Core Desired Feelings]

_____ requires me to **be less . . .**
[insert Core Desired Feelings]

In order to feel _____, I am **trusting that . . .**
                  [insert Core Desired Feelings]

In order to feel _____, I am **letting go of thoughts and beliefs that . . .**
                  [insert Core Desired Feelings]

In order to feel _____, I am **allowing for . . .**
                  [insert Core Desired Feelings]

In order to feel _____, I am **praying for . . . .**
                  [insert Core Desired Feelings]

INNER WORLD: ENCOURAGEMENT

Like all communication, it's often THE TONE that makes the difference—and the tone that you take with yourself is so important.

> ### Guidance
>
> Cheerlead yourself. Lead your own way. Create your reality with your mind. There are two ways to generate that type of bolstering optimism. First, there are **beliefs that we declare.** For example, *I am loved by God no matter what I do.* Or, *countless people have gone before me and healed and turned their lives around. I am doing the same.* Or, *joy is my natural state of being.*
>
> Second, there is **encouragement that we allow ourselves to receive from external sources.** Wisdom keepers, deities, and philosophers we admire. What would Spirit tell you? Or the Four Noble Truths of the Buddha? Your favourite prayer? The one-liner from a mystic that resonates with and guides you into the clear?
>
> Whether you are self-talking or drawing on another's wisdom, **what you hear is full of love and compassion, free of doubt or demands, and completely supportive of your goodness, strength, and fulfillment.**

MY DECLARATIONS + ENCOURAGEMENTS

INNER WORLD: DO/EXPERIENCE + HAVE/GIVE

Your Core Desired Feelings guide what you set out to achieve.

Guidance

You're building bridges from your heart to the outer world.

> **Go through each of the life areas and ask yourself what you want to do/experience + have/give in each area.** But you're going to do it from a fresh mindset—with your Core Desired Feelings guiding you, which is the opposite of how we've been socially trained to organize our lives. Typically we'd be aiming to "own a two-bedroom house," with the hope that we'd feel some form of fulfillment when we got it. But that's backwards. We work from the inside out now.

Cues

Do: *Actions, making, projects. Create. Start, stop, continue.*

Experience: *Partake in, be involved in, achieve, join. Grow, evolve. See.*

Have: *Own, get, buy, earn.*

Give: *Offer, lend, contribute, donate, gift.*

In **LIVELIHOOD + LIFESTYLE**, in order to feel _____
[insert your CDFs]

I want to **do/experience** . . .

I want to **have** . . .

I want to **give** . . .

In **BODY + WELLNESS**, in order to feel _____
[insert your CDFs]

I want to **do/experience** . . .

I want to **have** . . .

I want to **give** . . .

In **CREATIVITY + LEARNING**, in order to feel _____
[insert your CDFs]

I want to **do/experience** . . .

I want to **have** . . .

I want to **give** . . .

In **RELATIONSHIPS + SOCIETY**, in order to feel _____
[insert your CDFs]

I want to **do/experience** . . .

I want to **have** . . .

I want to **give** . . .

In **ESSENCE + SPIRITUALITY**, in order to feel _____
[insert your CDFs]

I want to **do/experience** . . .

I want to **have** . . .

I want to **give** . . .

In a few more steps, you're going to turn these outer world desires into intentions or goals. If some of these desires jump out as obvious to-do's, you can start to flesh out plans to actualize:

HOT LIST for do/experience + have/give

Do/experience + have/give:	Take action, notes to self, ideas, people:	By when:

OUTER WORLD: STOP DOING

In terms of creating your ideal life, what you decide to stop doing is as important as what you start doing.

Guidance

What's got to stop in order for you to feel the way you truly want to feel? You may want to refer back to your "what's not working" section because you've probably spelled out a lot of what needs to be retired.

There are two layers to this: the obvious and the deeper.

THE DEEPER. It can be hard to see how we sabotage our own happiness. That's the nature of self-sabotage. It's a destructive behaviour that tends to be unconscious—hidden from our full awareness.

Unearthing these patterns can require long term introspection, and some good coaching or counseling can help us get clear. But let's see what we can shake loose here and now.

So bring to mind your most loving, wise, and trusted friend or relative—they're in your life now or they've passed on. Or, imagine a spirit guide, or a Wise Elder, or the luminous and all-compassionate Divine Mother. You feel love and trust in their presence. And if you do have that kind of living voice of loving reason in your life, you could always just ask them directly. That's what friends are for.

Now just ask them: **What can I stop doing now in order to create more ease and joy in my life?** And listen. You might hear an answer word for word, you might have an idea. You may feel it in your heart. It doesn't have to be epic and loud. It's a gentle conversation with a friend who is making a great suggestion to you.

Now you commit to some action, or inaction, as the case may be.

Cues

Sell, give away. Delegate, reassign. Put an end to. Retire. Cancel. Delete. Burn. Phase out. Immediate halt. End. Over. Let go. Release. No more. Complete. Thank you, move on. Change.

In **LIVELIHOOD + LIFESTYLE,** to feel _____ I am **going to stop . . .**
[insert your CDFs]

In **BODY + WELLNESS,** to feel _____ I am **going to stop . . .**
[insert your CDFs]

In **CREATIVITY + LEARNING,** to feel _____ I am **going to stop . . .**
[insert your CDFs]

In **RELATIONSHIPS + SOCIETY,** to feel _____ I am **going to stop . . .**
[insert your CDFs]

In **ESSENCE + SPIRITUALITY,** to feel _____ I am **going to stop . . .**
[insert your CDFs]

In **LIVELIHOOD + LIFESTYLE,** to feel _____ I am **going to let go of . . .**
[insert your CDFs]

In **BODY + WELLNESS,** to feel _____ I am **going to let go of . . .**
[insert your CDFs]

In **CREATIVITY + LEARNING,** to feel _____ I am **going to let go of . . .**
[insert your CDFs]

In **RELATIONSHIPS + SOCIETY,** to feel _____ I am **going to let go of . . .**
[insert your CDFs]

In **ESSENCE + SPIRITUALITY,** to feel _____ I am **going to let go of . . .**
[insert your CDFs]

PART 3:

PLANNING
WITH YOUR CORE DESIRED FEELINGS

DREAM ANALYSIS

Let your dreams change with you.

> ### Guidance
>
> Look back. Do a reverie review. Consider your life *before* you named your Core Desired Feelings. Think both in terms of monumental dreams and specific goals. We're going to shine some light on the reasons behind the goals.

Write down three to five of the most memorable goals or aspirations you've taken on in the past few years. Career goals, wellness goals, relationship desires, creative aspirations—whatever you wanted to achieve.

Then hold each of those achievables up to the following questions:

What motivated you to take this on? (And if you're in a group of trusted friends, go ahead—ask them why they think you took this on. Their insight might surprise you.)

How did you think you were going to feel when you reached your goal?

How did you feel while you were pursuing this goal?

What did you tell yourself about yourself when you accomplished, or didn't accomplish, this goal?

Do you still think about this resolution? If so, how does it feel to think about it now?

MEASURE. Here's a very big, but very simple question: **Do your dreams and goals help you feel your Core Desired Feelings?**

Here's an example. Let's say one of your past goals was to lose weight to see a specific number on the scale. So you restricted yourself from some of your favourite foods. You declined invites to gatherings with friends because you didn't want to be tempted by the calories in drinks and food. Your attention was on constraint, constraint, constraint. So you felt . . . constrained.

Now your intention shifts from the scale to your Core Desired Feelings. Your new CDFs are Light, Strong, Freedom—all of which are the opposite of constraint. The goal shifts to feeling the way you want to feel, not your weight on the scale. So you drop the restrictive dieting and make food and fitness choices that make you feel Light, Strong, and Freedom. (BTW, we've heard this story many times in the Desire Map Community.)

Look at each dream/goal and ask yourself:

How does having this dream or going after this goal currently make me feel?

Does the dream or goal make me feel expanded? Is it pulling me forward? Am I 100% enthusiastic about it? Or . . . does it make me feel constricted, obligated, weighed down?

Which dreams/goals are aligned with which of your Core Desired Feelings? Let me ask that another way: **when you picture that dream coming true, in that future scenario are you clearly feeling one or more of your CDFs?**

STEP 1:
Pre-existing dreams for my life:

STEP 2:
Current feelings about the dream/goal.
Check all that apply:

☐ Expansive	☐ Enthusiastic	☐ Capable
☐ Resourced	☐ Pressured	☐ Heavy
☐ Stressed	☐ Scared	☐ It's complicated

☐ Expansive	☐ Enthusiastic	☐ Capable
☐ Resourced	☐ Pressured	☐ Heavy
☐ Stressed	☐ Scared	☐ It's complicated

☐ Expansive	☐ Enthusiastic	☐ Capable
☐ Resourced	☐ Pressured	☐ Heavy
☐ Stressed	☐ Scared	☐ It's complicated

☐ Expansive	☐ Enthusiastic	☐ Capable
☐ Resourced	☐ Pressured	☐ Heavy
☐ Stressed	☐ Scared	☐ It's complicated

GOAL VETTING BEFORE GOAL SETTING

Still want it? Want it more than ever? Okay, then . . .

> **Guidance**
>
> Refer to your DO/EXPERIENCE + HAVE/GIVE lists. Look at the dreams and goals you just assessed. Now it's up to your heart to make the call on what you're going to focus on creating and achieving in the near future. It all comes back to enthusiasm!

The most powerful question to ask yourself when you consider which intentions or goals to focus on is: **WHAT AM I MOST EXCITED ABOUT?** That's the key. This is about what lights you up the most. It's about what thrills you. Never mind that it may also be daunting and unreasonable. What are you most enthusiastic about? Enthusiasm vibrates at a higher level of consciousness.

Your CDFs	Your dreams, goals, intentions that will help you feel your CDFs

Hold these questions up to your potential intentions + goals:

How will this affect other people?

How can I work with people I like to get this done?

Does this help me generate more than one of my Core Desired Feelings?

How would I feel if I died without doing this?

What will take the least amount of effort to pull off?

What has the highest earning potential?

What will require the largest amount of money?

How could this affect the next five to ten years of my life?

What is the scariest thing to do?

Do I feel I was born to do this?

INTENTION + GOAL SETTING

Envision. Give it over to Life. Repeat.

YEARLY INTENTIONS + GOALS: Here's my theory. Significant intentions can often take time to achieve. And a year flies by, so you have to *focus*. It might ache a bit to put some intentions on the back burner. Naturally. But you can circle back to those with some energy later. The momentum and satisfaction you'll gain from pulling off just a few amazing endeavors will outweigh the gain of doing a bunch of things halfway.

Set out to do three or four things over a year with ease and excellence, rather than doing a dozen things just sufficiently.

CHOOSE LESS IF YOU NEED TO: And hey, if you're aiming to do something stupendous this year, then by all means, make that your singular focus. This could be The Year of the Concert Tour; The Year We Built the House; The Year I Got a Promotion; The Year of Healing; The Year I Finished My Book.

Guidance

This is where you sift through everything that you said you want to do, experience, have, and give in your life—and you choose the most important of those intentions. Keep this really simple because it's really profound.

And remember: Everything is progress. The universe is always expanding—that includes you. Errors, missteps, detours—it's all progress. You can change your mind, anytime. Just like that.

Just keep your energy moving. Motion is usually better than stasis. Of course there are times to retreat and be still and wait. But that's INTENTIONAL, ACTIVE waiting—energy is still flowing because you're not in fear. When you stay still because you're afraid to make a move, your self-worth wanes, your doubts fester and breed more doubts, your courage atrophies. It's not pretty. Suit up and head out. When you take action, you learn, you build skills, you become freer.

MY INTENTIONS . . .

BRUTAL FACTS + FEARS

Bring fear to your consciousness so it can be addressed, healed, and released.

> ## Guidance
>
> Head down to the basement of your psyche where you store the gnarly fears and unresolved hurts, and take a look around at what's in there. When we look directly at our fears and perceived limitations, we move them from the subconscious (where they can control us), to our consciousness (where we have more agency and wisdom). See it so you can be in charge of it. Acknowledge your fears so you can put your loving attention on them, your compassion and understanding. *That's* how you change fear and resentment into clarity and freedom.

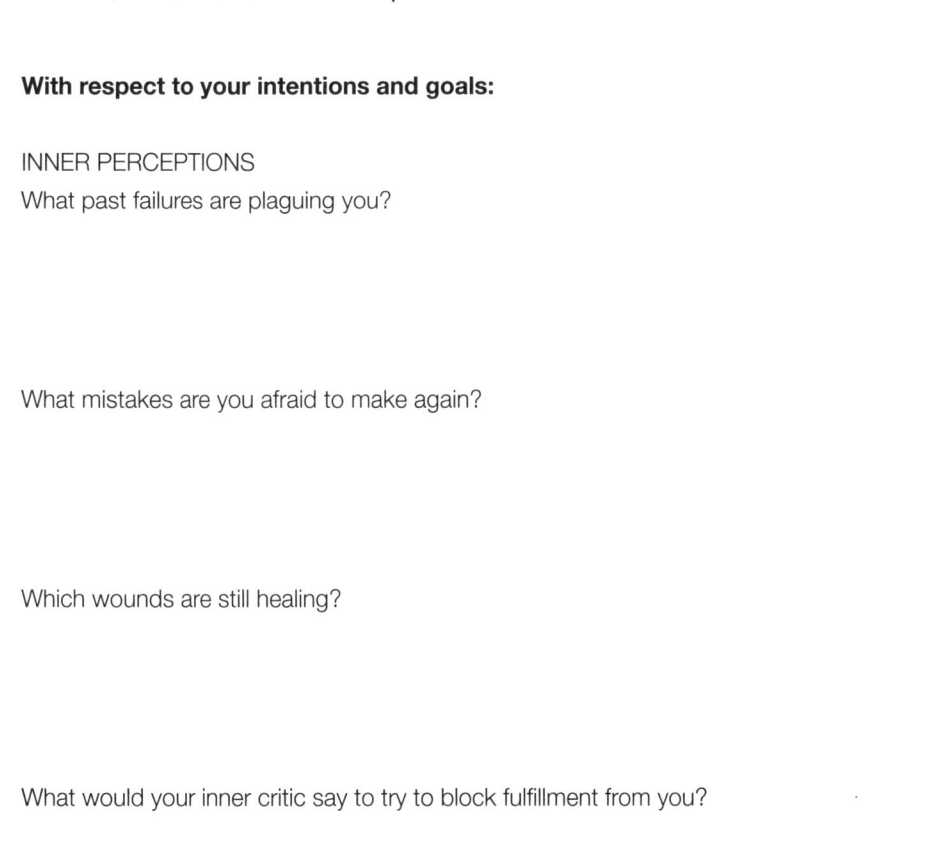

With respect to your intentions and goals:

INNER PERCEPTIONS
What past failures are plaguing you?

What mistakes are you afraid to make again?

Which wounds are still healing?

What would your inner critic say to try to block fulfillment from you?

INNER PERCEPTIONS

What are the current tough circumstances, market conditions, or possible obstacles on the way to your fulfilled intentions and goals? Note: these aren't your fears. These are more likely outer world facts.

What are your current healthy commitments and wholeheartedly-chosen obligations (not the resented obligations that you want to get out of).

What are your current limits? All of which can be overcome and morph over time, but they do need to be factored in at this moment. When we honour our limits, rather than pretending they don't exist or that we should just plow over them, we remove the stress of goal-chasing and we can work more gracefully from the present.

What are you inspired to rise above and transform? Yes to being in the Flow of life, yes. And sometimes there's another form of self-care: doing whatever it takes.

LOVE NOTE: Get ready to make changes for your future without criticizing your past. Don't burn energy on analyzing the shit out of your mistakes or setbacks. You need that energy to make some changes and get creative. How you regard your present and past can influence how your future unfolds.

Coming up next!

In THE DESIRE MAP MANUAL FOR LIVING you'll find a visualization practice for manifesting. It's layered, and potentially powerful, if you use it. And your intentions and goals are going to love it.

THE DESIRE MAP

MANUAL FOR LIVING

AKA PART 4:

LIVING

YOUR CORE DESIRED FEELINGS

KEY PRACTICES

THE HEART-CENTERING PRACTICE

Return to your heart and bring your Core Desired Feelings to life.
Breathing is the way home. Heart-focused breathing fills that home with love and clarity.

The HEART-CENTERING Practice combines mindfulness with heartfulness, wrapped in the power of breath and prayer. We greet our Life Source and take a witnessing view of current and desired feelings. We verbalize self-compassion, tune into our life force, apply the medicine of gratitude and colour and light. Then activate our self-agency by attuning to the wisdom of our Core Desired Feelings—and acting on them.

The touchstone sentence to recall the steps:

With **Breathing, Feeling + Compassion,** *I am* **Presence**. *With* **Gratitude** *I choose my* **Core Desired Feelings** *in* **thought and action.**

SET UP:

1. Focus all of your attention **directly on your heart center** for the entire practice. You may feel an aching, warmth, or expansion . . . that's *aliveness*.

2. Inhale and exhale **through your nose,** keep your mouth gently closed. Breathe **slowly, a little more deeply** than you normally would.

3. Before you begin, **know how you are going to greet your Higher Power.** I suggest, "Hello, God." Other suggestions: *Father Mother God. Spirit. Creation. Life.* And rather than Hello, you could also begin with *Thank You* or *I Feel You* . . .

4. Before you begin, know which **Core Desired Feeling(s)** you will bring into your heart. Or you can go with whatever comes to mind at that place in the practice.

The 7 Heart-Centering steps:

Breathe.

If you feel inclined, gently place your left hand on your chest, covered by your right hand.

Inhale from your heart and say, "Hello, God." Exhale from your heart and say, "I'm here." Do that as many times as you like, then shift gears: deeply inhale one whole breath for five steady counts. 1-2-3-4-5. Fully exhale at the same pace of five counts. 5-4-3-2-1.

Feel.

Observe what you're feeling in this moment. "I'm happy," or "I'm sad." Phrase it as a witness: *"I feel happiness,"* or *"I'm experiencing sadness."*

A variety of feelings may come into your consciousness. Happiness, anxiety, joy, fear, peace, worry, gratitude. You may have one or two predominant feelings. Let them all float into your awareness. Just notice.

Compassion.

Say something deeply kind and encouraging to yourself, or imagine it being said to you by a great being. Suggestions: *I matter. I'm valued. I am deeply loved.* Or . . . *You're safely held. You are beloved. You're incredibly resilient and wise. You deserve joy and peace. The flow of life is carrying you.*

Gratitude.

Name something you're grateful for and bask in that feeling of appreciation. You can make a gratitude statement to yourself, *"I give thanks for . . ." "I am grateful . . ."* Be in the sensation of gratitude.

Presence.

Be still and notice the life force that's pulsing within you. If it helps, you can simply focus on one area of your physical body, such as your hands or your heart center. Be aware of the subtle energy that's there, it's a steady, radiant pulse. Keep breathing through your heart.

Breathe a Core Desired Feeling into your heart.

Bring one or more CDFs into your heart's awareness and sense it unfolding in your heart with each breath. Visualize luminous colours of **light pink, milky white,** and **translucent gold** circulating in your heart center. Your Core Desired Feeling(s) is intermingling with the pinks, white, and gold, and that feeling is filling your heart.

Ask that feeling(s) if it has an image or some **guidance** to give you. Continue breathing with your heart center.

Choose a life-affirming thought and action.

Decide on **one encouraging thought and one action** that reflects that Core Desired Feeling(s). Breathe that loving direction into your heart. Give thanks, always. Take a few deep breaths and open your eyes.

CREATE A CORE DESIRED FEELINGS BLESSING

A single word, in any language, spoken with sacred intention can become a blessing. Words are part of the cosmic fabric. They have a vibration. Used with awareness, mantras or "Words of Power" or "Blessings" can help us return to balance. They can heal us, protect us, and be used as tools for creating.

Your Core Desired Feelings can become your blessing words.

Creating your own word blessing: First, you're going to put your sacred intention and energy in to each word. You're going to "power up" your words by infusing them with energy.

Visualize. Close your eyes and breathe fully with your heart center. Cup your hands together in front of you, like you would to hold water in your hands. Then see each Core Desired Feeling as a luminous, golden seed in your palms.

For each seed, take a deep breath in and on the exhale speak the name of each Core Desire Feeling into each individual golden seed. You're breathing energy into each word. Take your time, let your slow and deep breathing set the pace, you're acknowledging the truth, beauty, and power of each CDF word.

Then, bring your palms to your chest and place the seeds into the center of your heart. Your heart is filled with golden light. As the seeds soak in this luminosity, each one cracks open and blossoms into a bigger orb of golden light. Again, name and acknowledge each orb with its Core Desired Feeling word. Slowly, very deliberately. You're juicing up every word. Each feeling is receiving the blessing of your Love and is harmonizing with who you are.

Now ask your Higher Power to bless your power words: *Dear Father Mother God (Life, Spirit, Guides . . .) Please nourish, love, and protect these seeds of Light:* (with strong intention, name each Core Desired Feeling.)

Conclude with a few deep breaths and thanks.

WORD BLESSING PRACTICE

Now for putting your Core Desired Feelings Blessing into regular practice. Recite your CDFs as a focusing and revitalizing blessing as often as you like. Ideal times: when waking up and before sleep. So simple. Focus your love on those words and speak each one silently to yourself or aloud. Say them in the bath. Whisper them before a meeting or call. Sing them in the car. Loop them in your mind while you exercise. The unconscious picks up on and starts to believe every word you say. Feed it life-affirming cues.

You are affecting your reality with these words of power. You are directing your subconscious to a positive reality. These words are your wands.

You can speak your CDF Blessing just once, with all you've got to give, or repeat it twenty-one times with your eyes closed, or three times while you're brushing your teeth—whatever works.

A powerful time to recite your Core Desired Feelings is first thing in the morning and before you fall asleep for the night—perfect times for your subconscious to be attended to.

You can state your CDFs as an affirmation or a prayer. I highly recommend doing this as a repetitive writing exercise. For example, choose one of these lead-in phrases, fill in your CDFs, and write out the full statement three to twelve times.

And instead of saying to yourself, "I want to feel Connection," or "I want to feel Radiance," you might want to use affirmative phrasing: "I am Connection," and "I am Radiance." You can use affirmative and wishing phrases interchangeably, depending on your head and heart space.

Suggested Affirmative + Prayer Statements

I am . . . [Core Desired Feelings]

Thank you . . . [Core Desired Feelings]

Please guide me to be . . . [Core Desired Feelings]

Today I see . . . [Core Desired Feelings]

I receive . . . [Core Desired Feelings]

I give . . . [Core Desired Feelings]

I create . . . [Core Desired Feelings]

I move as . . . [Core Desired Feelings]

I am creating abundance with . . . [Core Desired Feelings]

I am connecting through . . . [Core Desired Feelings]

I am serving with . . . [Core Desired Feelings]

I am healing with . . . [Core Desired Feelings]

FUTURE PRESENT

Here's a beautiful notion to consider: You already have a lot of what you want, in places you may have overlooked, in different packaging than you may have expected, and hidden in plain sight.

Appreciate the indirect ways in which Life is already delivering on your dreams.

WHAT DO YOU WANT . . . THAT YOU ALREADY HAVE? Review what you want to do/experience + have/give. Choose a few desires to focus on for this exercise. With each one, look at where you already have that quality, feeling, or experience in your life—you might have to dig deep to find it. That's okay. Even if it's just a subtle sensation, you'll find it somewhere.

For example, let's say you want to laugh more with your significant other. It's part of your deeper craving for more intimacy and joy. Currently, you're not laughing much with your person and you're feeling sad and getting bitter about it. The pressure is on for some delight to happen. Understandable.

Let's try to alleviate some of that intense craving. Someone in your life must be filling your funny cup.

You already have your best girlfriend who makes you laugh your ass off at least once a week. And dude at work is good for some champion sarcasm every day. So note to self: Call your bestie more, thank her for sparking your joy, and let work dude know that he's a comic genius. Focus on the laughter that you do have in your life, even if it's not currently from the direct source that you want it from. Take the pressure off the object of your craving for a minute.

See the positivity already flowing through your life. Resist the temptation to compare it to what you're lacking in other areas of your life. Just keep appreciating, appreciating, appreciating what's working, where it's working.

Why? Because this practice of clear seeing and gratitude comforts your nervous system. And when your nervous system calms down, you can make better choices and respond more fully to every situation in your life. This practice is not only soothing, but it can also help you to lighten the eff up.

A few more examples:

> "I want an additional $500 every pay period." You want more money to flow to you. What do you want that you already have? "I got money back from income taxes! I get a paid holiday next week. Now that I work at home on Fridays, I save a hundred bucks a month on train fare and lunch out. Affirmative note to self: My money and energy flow is increasing." You just found about five hundred additional dollars in your life. More is sure to come, very possibly from sources you haven't even accounted for yet.

"I want to spend more time in nature. I'm stuck in a cubicle, in a big city, and I'm going bonkers. Plus I can't get out of town right now." What do you want that you already have? "Well, I'm bringing flowers in to work this week. Sleeping with the bedroom windows open. I'm sitting on my balcony to say prayers every night before bed. I'm framing those photos from my holiday in the Sierras. Action note to self: Book that hiking trip in Maine NOW. No excuses." Small acts of self-care can boost the bigger choices required to go after your desires—like moving out of the city.

"I want a good friend to tell my dreams to." What do you want that you already have? "I already have my journal; my dog and my deaf grandma are all great listeners. I can tell them anything and everything about my dreams and they don't judge me. Affirmative note to self: Even if I don't have a best friend who gets me, Life hears my dreams. Every single one."

Sometimes a stretch, but it's exercising your heart. This is the kind of self-empowerment that starts to rinse away any lurking victim mentality. Start somewhere.

Here's what happens when you find evidence of fulfillment and pleasure in your current reality:

You take the desperation out of your wants and needs, you will think more clearly and act more calmly. Because you're appreciating more in your life, you'll cling less to what you want—and that lighter touch helps your creative energy flow. Things can come to you more easily when you're feeling lighter. You ease up on the people around you. You generate gratitude—which is a transformative force. And you might realize that you—and some of the people you love, are further along than you've been giving yourself or them credit for. A lot in your life and relationships is working.

The future you desire is showing up in your present. Grow it with gratitude.

What I desire to feel + have now and in the future . . . *more, new, greater, more fun, shinier, deeper, fuller . . .*	Where, when, how some of that is already present in my life (in ANY form, from ANY source, in ANY amount . . .)

THE DESIRE MAP MANIFESTING PRACTICE

Believe it to see it.

1. COME FROM THE HEART: We intend to create from the heart and soul.

We have a heart-centered vision. This vision arises from deep love of the interconnected self and others—a place of intrinsic fusion with all Life. It's compassionate, it's joyful, and it feels connected to everyone else. A heart-centered vision benefits the whole collective.

Heart-centered visions arise from a place of awareness and Light. Ego-centered visions arise from the shadow. Ego-based visions may come from a place of lacking, and having to prove something, which ultimately creates division within ourselves and the people around us. Ego-based dreams are often about needing to achieve something in order to feel "worthy."

A heart-centered vision is a celebration of our inherent soul nature. It is rooted in higher values—values that help uplift all involved—love, wisdom, abundance, generosity, healing, joy that ripples out. A vision that comes from Love is deeply nourishing and interdependent.

A heart-centered vision helps unite your inner and your outer world: you're invoking your Core Desired Feelings (inner) and allowing them to manifest into reality (outer).

2) HAVE FAITH . . . AND ACT ON IT.

> "Faith is the substance of things hoped for, the evidence of things not seen."
> — Hebrews 11

Faith is believing that the Light exists, even when it's dark. You can't prove it then and there, but you know in the deepest part of your being, of its existence. You have Faith. So with respect to manifesting, we're fostering the Faith that our desires will be made manifest. Doubt is a choice. Faith is a choice. Choose Faith.

But Faith alone isn't enough. You have to meet God with some action in this dimension. Another reference from the Bible to make the point, from James 2:14 "What does it profit, my brethren, if someone says he has faith but does not have works? Can faith save him? If a brother or sister is naked and destitute of daily food, and one of you says to them, 'Depart in peace, be warmed and filled,' but you do not give them the things which are needed for the body, what does it profit? Thus also faith by itself, if it does not have works, is dead." Back up that Faith with some action. Faith on its own is . . . useless. Faith requires care and feeding.

Faith is like a blueprint of what you want to build. It's a track that you lay down in the substratum that the vision will grow through and rise. The "work" involved, the building on that blue print of Faith, is the work of inner and outer devotion. Keep your heart and mind and body clean and clear. Be diligent to stay well and vital. Keep removing the obstacles to Love and let it flow into the world. Purify and give. Purify and give. And repeat— THAT's the work that brings Faith to life.

1. AND NOW . . . VISUALIZE.

Working with visualizations is a metaphysical science and an art. Visualize the fulfillment of your desire—a punctuated moment that says it all. So for example, you want to win a medal, you're not seeing yourself training to win the race, you're seeing yourself—and feeling yourself, victorious on the podium. It's a completion scenario. Think about the best possible outcome of your goals and intentions and deepest desires, and that's the scene.

You're going to create **two or three individual, simple visions**—power vignettes. Of course, in each vision you are FEELING your Core Desired Feelings. Basking in them. Embodying them. The feelings are the SPICE, they make a difference. They're magnetic.

Once you decide on the final visual that you want to bring to life, treat it like a "seed" that has to be nurtured daily for its gestation period. Just like a fertilized egg in the womb from inception until it's ready to be delivered. So once you craft that vision, keep nourishing it daily.

If you're really committed, then 21 minutes of visualization time is megafertilizer. Super devoted? Do this consistently for nine months to a year. Hold the vision in Faith, with your Core Desired Feelings in your heart. The very commitment of that practice is going to pay off in multiple ways.

This an important metaphysical side note: don't keep changing the vision. It's like changing your dinner order in a restaurant a bunch of times—the confusion means you don't get a good meal on time. Craft your visualization. Trust it. And work with it.

Suggestions on the vision themes (these are only suggestions):

One scene that encapsulates the **greater reality** you want. Your ideal life. Your current, deep desire.

One scene encapsulates your **wellness and vitality.**

One scene encapsulates your **abundance and/or work in the world.**

See, sense, hear, smell it: where you are, who you are with, the quality of light and air, the sounds that you hear, your sensory nature is active and alive.

FEEL it: As you're seeing the vision, breathe your Core Desired Feelings through your heart.

Add colour: Infuse your Core Desired Feelings with light pink, white light, and translucent golds.

Give thanks. Go on to the next vision.

After your visualization, release the vision. Send it into the sky, the ethers, pure space, until it fully disappears from your sight. Now let your faith handle it for you. You don't need to obsess about it all day. You focus on Faith—purifying and giving, and generating your Core Desired Feelings in your daily current reality.

Always conclude with thanks. Give thanks to all the Beings, seen and unseen, who are helping you manifest your vision into reality.

MY 2 OR 3 VISIONS:
(Write this as a simple description of your fulfilled desire moment.)

GRATITUDE + FAITH PRACTICES

EVEN DEEPER GRATITUDE

Gratitude is a muscle to strengthen and to sculpt. You want to practice it regularly, but bring in a fresh approach once and a while. This practice helps you strrretch your appreciative heart and mind. It's great to do as a writing reflection.

    1. What am I **taking for granted** this week? (Sunrise, breath, electricity. A reliable partner/relative, loving pets.)

    2. Who helps to keep the **comforts** of my life coming to me? (Loved ones, colleagues, professionals, service and product providers near and far.)

    3. What **systems** are helping my life to run right now? (Social structures, civil services, networks, technology, groups.)

    4. Three **mundane** things that I do almost daily that I'm grateful for (be sure to articulate why you're grateful for them).

    5. Five **utilitarian** things I use in my life, why I'm grateful for them, and some of the factors and circumstances that help bring those into my life. (Phone, clean drinking water, transit, clothes.)

BUILDING ON GRATITUDE

This one's so much fun. Riff off five to ten situations that you are grateful for in your life right now.

Choose the three gratitudes that are most vibrant for you. For each one, come up with ideas to either celebrate, honour, give thanks for, or create even more of that situation in your life.

PUBLIC GRATITUDE

The How-Tos of Small, Specific, Genuine—and Publicly Declared—Gratitude.

1. Post to social media as the spirit moves you.

2. Only express gratitude if it's genuine. Do NOT post "just to get something on Facebook" or for recognition.

3. See the obvious gifts of the day. And then . . .

4. Look for what you might be taking for granted. So many of us have systems of love and consciousness, governance and privilege that underpin our everyday lives. What and who keeps your life running?

5. The profound and the seemingly trivial live side by side in the day-to-day. Put it all in the mix.

6. Personally, I use "Life" as a term to cover God, Goddess, the Cosmos, Nature—all of it. Thank whatever greater force you most relate to.

7. Even if your day, your week, your year has sucked, dig to find something to appreciate. Did you have to walk to get clean water today? Do you have a telephone? Does one person on the planet love you just a little bit? Are you still here? Muster it if you have to. You'll feel better. You will inspire someone.

Envision this: For every piece of negative news that is broadcast, for every snarky-critical tweet and gossipy link . . . a hundred instances of Small, Specific, Genuine (and Publicly Declared) Gratitude. Here's to a revolution!

RATIOS OF GRATITUDE

This week, every time you declare 1 negative about your life, your neighbor, your society . . . counter it with 7 gratefuls.

> 1 complaint, then 7 thank yous.
> 1 pain point, then 7 pleasurables.
> 1 despair, then 7 joys.

This is important: Don't try to "battle" or beat down the negatives with your positives. We don't want to create dueling realties. That's a silly New Age concept. The negatives are just as valuable as the positives. Just decide where you're going to focus. One dissatisfaction, fine. Seven gratitudes, even more fine.

"WHAT I TRUST" LIST

Before a supercharged opportunity, I do a trust ritual with myself. Often we're so busy trying to get our endorphins fired up to go get 'em!, we can forget that feeling assured is a strong state of being.

Sometimes you have doubts, and legit reasons to be cautious—and you're going for it anyway. That's the definition of courage. And it's easier to be brave when you can reference all that's strong and well in your life.

>1. **Focus on the present.** The point of this exercise is to access the trust that you already have. It's unwavering and true for you. This is not about building new trust or visualizing outcomes. We're concentrating on what is currently working.
>
>2. **Write it out.** It's important that your "What I Trust" List be written out, not typed up. The movement, hand to vision, helps your psyche to feel the comfort. Imagine your mind is like a lung, inhaling and exhaling as you list out what your trusting. And/or . . .
>
>3. **Speak it out.** If you're an auditory-learner, speak it out. Leave yourself a voicemail, or record a voice memo on your mobile, or talk to yourself. Kindly.
>
>4. **Stream your consciousness.** Just let it pour out—but, again, don't include things on your list that you don't fully have trust in. It's okay if your list is short—brevity is better than bravado. For example: *I trust my love for my sweetheart. I trust my integrity. I trust how much my mom loves me. I trust that my Guides are watching out for me. I trust how much I deeply love my children. I trust that he'll be there when I call. I trust that my best friend will always be there for me. I trust that there's always another idea. I trust that I can always get a job. I trust that my car will be there when I get back.*
>
>5. **Be really obvious if you need to be.** Nothing is too great or too small to put your trust in. Sometimes the most basic things will give you a boost, especially if you're finding it difficult to think of things that you fully trust in. *I trust my next breath will keep coming. I trust the sun will rise tomorrow. I trust Sparky will be wagging his tail when I walk in the door. I trust that the snow will melt.*

Trust now. Trust in the Now. Consciously access what you know to be positively true. That sureness strengthens the bridge to what's next.

REFRAMING PRACTICES

ALIGN YOUR THOUGHTS

Change your thoughts and you change your feelings.

It can be difficult to bridge how we feel in the moment—especially when the circumstance feels negative—to how we want to feel (our CDFs).

We can't always change our circumstances, but there's always a way to generate more life-affirming feelings. We can get to our CDFs by changing our perspective about the circumstance itself, which then liberates us to start activating more of the feelings we actually want to feel.

As an example, let's consider someone who loathes their job (I've heard this countless times over the years from people in our online community). Let's say that they can't leave their job in the immediate future, they have expenses and commitments. Enter Desire Mapping, they get clear on their CDFs, they set a soulful goal to eventually leave that crap job. But for now, they've got to stick it out.

So rather than feeling resentment or constriction in their job: how can they feel their Core Desired Feelings even in this less than ideal situation? **They can start to think different thoughts—more positive and grateful thoughts that will nourish their Core Desired Feelings.** This is a *daily* practice for all of us.

It can empower us to feel our CDFs in current time, even before our less than ideal circumstances change. This means less personal suffering, more energy for turning toward higher vibration feelings.

You can do this as a mental exercise or a written reflection.

1. **How are you feeling?** The positive and negative. Write it out or review it in your mind.

2. **What are you thinking?** The positive and negative.

3. **Choose one of the feelings that you do not want to be having. Correlate that feeling to your thinking.** Ask yourself: What thoughts am I thinking that are influencing this feeling? *i.e. I hate my job. I'm stuck in this situation.*

4. Recall one or all of your **Core Desired Feelings**—how you *do* want to be feeling.

5. **What life-affirming, healthy thoughts can you choose that are aligned with the energy of your CDF(s)?** i.e. *"I'm grateful that this job income is giving me the security to follow my creative passions in my own time while I plan for the future." "I had the power to get this job, I have the power to get another job." "I'm choosing to be here, I'm acting from my own free will and my love and care for myself and my family."*

PRESENT WITH THE NEGATIVE

"Negative" feelings are part of the human experience. There's no plainer or profound way to put that. To deny the negative feelings is to resist the power of our presence—we miss out on life. Pushing away the darkness can be a precursor to numbing out and all kinds of addiction. We have to lean in.

And, we often learn through contrast. That's part of living in a dualistic reality. Restriction can lead to freedom. Shame can lead to pride. Weakness can lead to integrity. Again, lean in.

So let's look at our willingness to experience the more difficult emotions. It's important to note that a "negative" feeling doesn't have to be regarded as a "bad" or weakening experience. Anger can be creative, sorrow can bring us closer to life. But for these purposes, "negative" feelings are what most of us would relate to as heavy, uncomfortable, painful . . . negative.

We're also aiming to understand why some feelings are easier and more difficult to experience than others. This way, when a negative feeling arises, you can see its associations and make a clearer choice to return to encouraging thoughts and your Core Desired Feelings.

Negative feelings that I can experience with **openness and intention.** (i.e. Sadness, doubt, confusion, anger) . . .

Why I'm able to experience those negative feelings with openness and intention . . .

Negative feelings that **I can be comfortable** experiencing. (i.e. Fear, uncertainty, overwhelm, melancholy, jealousy) . . .

Why I'm able to be comfortable experiencing those negative feelings . . .

Negative feelings that have been **extremely difficult** for me to experience (they are CDF blockers). (i.e. Shame, anxiety, depression, apathy, unworthiness) . . .

Why those negative feelings are extremely difficult for me to experience . . .

FEELING ANTICIPATION

Looming, planned, or about to take place. Think of some near to far future situations that you're anticipating . . . with a bit of dread or caution—and decide ahead of time that you'll get heart-centered. See yourself doing the Heart-Centering Practice with your breath and intention.

Write out two or three potentially challenging situations that you could encounter and ask yourself how your Core Desired Feelings would respond.

Potentially trying situation:	How would your CDFs respond?
When I mess up or don't hit a goal.	
Hanging out with my triggering relative.	
Awkward first meeting.	

FORWARD FOCUS

It's not fruitful to bypass painful feelings with contrived positive thoughts. You need to look directly at negative feelings. That said, even if you're profoundly discouraged, just using future-focused words can create a positive shift. When you're not feeling the way you want, you can say this: **"I'm really looking forward to feeling . . . [insert your Core Desired Feelings]**. Or this, "Well, at least I'm even clearer about how I want to feel now." Or perhaps all you can eke out is, "Maybe I'll be grateful for this someday." That's a step in the right direction.

Generate hope—it's a form of resiliency.

DEEPER LIVING PRACTICES

HOW WILL YOU GIVE OF YOURSELF?

Generous people have more to give. Living service of others is one of our greatest powers and sources of fulfillment. So how can you connect your Core Desired Feelings—that are all about YOU—to how you are of service in the world?

Where would you like to contribute your love, talent, and expertise in a way that will light you up? You don't have to commit to giving in all the ways that come to mind, you can turn some of this into an intention down the road. Just free flow about what's possible—it's usually an energy boost to look at where and how you can be the giver. Too often being of service can pull on our sense of duty, and certainly we are honour bound to serve on this planet. But contributing out of a heavy sense of obligation isn't sustainable or enriching. We want to serve from the fullness of our hearts. So look for connections between social issues and your life-affirming desires, your CDFs.

GIVING PROMPTS

How can you raise money, donate time and/or other resources, raise visibility and awareness of an issue, and serve in a way that elicits the best of you?

What would you like to revolutionize?

What causes are aligned with your Core Desired Feelings?

How can you be of service to:

    . . . the immediate people in your life

    . . . your local community

    . . . your industry

    . . . marginalized populations

    . . . children

    . . . humanity

    . . . animals

    . . . Mother Earth

    . . . the Universe

HELPFUL PEOPLE + RESOURCES

Desire Mapping is about exercising your individual capacity to feel the way you want to feel. And! We are in this together. We're here to serve the collective with our whole hearts. We need to turn to one another to ask for help. This is a great monthly exercise.

	People/groups who can help me live out my Core Desired Feelings	Loving request I'll make, offering of service, focused learning, turning to . . .
People who are local, near to me, who I know directly and personally . . .		
Professionals, experts, service providers . . .		
Wisdom keepers + teachers (include their writing, programs, courses) who I can call on, turn to, or learn from . . .		
Deities, angels, spirits, spiritual forces I can call on . . .		

QUALITIES + EXPRESSIONS REFLECTION

Choose one CDF this week to reflect on . . .

MY CDF _____

Acts like . . .

Takes care of itself . . .

Watches . . .

Comes from . . .

Creates . . .

Does NOT want . . .

Manifests . . .

Asks . . .

Says NO to . . .

Wears . . .

Celebrates . . .

Says YES to . . .

Eats . . .

Wishes for . . .

Spends . . .

Listens to . . .

Prays for . . .

Rests . . .

Reads . . .

Gives thanks for . . .

Believes in . . .

Wakes up . . .

Has friends who . . .

Goes to bed . . .

Loves . . .

STAY IN LOVE
with Your Core Desired Feelings

As a monthly or quarterly journaling or reflection exercise . . .

Ask these questions of each of your CDFs:

What does it **feel** like to be _____ ?
[insert CDF]

What does it **look** like to be _____ ?
[insert CDF]

What does it **sound** like to be _____ ?
[insert CDF]

INNER CHILD CHECK IN

Imagine yourself and your Inner Child in a grove of cherry trees in blossom. Just hanging, happily. Love them up with your own grown-up wisdom and clarity. Give them your full attention. They are pure LOVE.

Ask your younger self how they're doing these days. How do they want to be feeling? What CDFs are delighting them? What do they need more of from you?

SUPERHERO CHECK IN

Have a meeting on a private plane with your Superhero self. They show up for you, strong, robust, full of energy, and determination. PRESENT.

Ask your Inner Superhero how they want to approach the next few weeks and where your strengths are. What CDFs are they feeling energized by? What do they want to give you more of?

FUTURE SELF CHECK IN

See your Future Self standing at the end of a winding garden path. They are so happy to see you, with such a loving and knowing gaze. They are RADIANT.

Ask your Future Self what they want to tell you about your current growth . . . how far you've come and what you're learning. Ask them how to bring each of your CDFs to life in a way that will move you forward.

HUGS + A REMINDER

de·vo·tion

noun

1. love, loyalty, or enthusiasm for a person, activity, or cause
2. loyalty, faithfulness, fidelity, trueness, steadfastness, constancy, commitment, allegiance, dedication

Your Soul is requesting your devotion in this life and you are answering the call.

All the simple acts of tuning in to ourselves to attune with the Divine, that's devotion. It's a daily thing. A choice-by-choice thing. It's what we are made for, and why we are here.

Joy, growth, connection, service . . . these are the fruits of tending to our inner life, and this is how we are nourishing each other and the planet. We are doing this.

Keep tending to your deep sensitivity, your innate wellness, your quantum power. Let your breath return you to your heart. Choose that Love. And then be that . . . in all ways. Devoted.

You are loved. You are loving.

Love,

WHOLE LOTTA LOVE

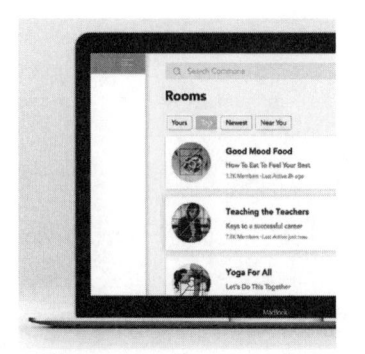

WeCommune.

ONLINE SUPPORT for DESIRE MAPPING and Beyond . . . a kindness-based online global community for wellness. And specifically for Desire Mapping guidance—from Danielle, Team D, a host of Desire Map Facilitator + Coaches, and one another. There are so many resources in this positive online platform—the best use of social platforms! Please come.

cmn.to/
DESIREMAP

BECOME A DESIRE MAP WORKSHOP FACILITATOR or COACH

Teach about Core Desired Feelings. If you're a coach, leader, or teacher in the making, we give you the tools to help your clients go deeper and flourish. This curriculum outlines multiple workshops—from a few hours to 3-day-long retreats—and coaching material to help your people return to their hearts through their Core Desired Feelings. As part of the licensing program, Team D and our superstar Facilitators offer ongoing wisdom for excellent facilitation skills, coaching, and marketing outreach.

TheDesireMap.com/
FACILITATOR

FREE + CLEAR ONLINE PROGRAM   COMMUNE

Review and reset your year. This is a prequel to *The Desire Map*—that you can do anytime. The beautiful video program and worksheets are an unconventional Year-In-Review process to help you look at the highs, lows, learnings, and yearnings of your recent past. It's the kind of reset that brings you closer to your Soul. And with that clarity comes more powerful choices—heart-driven choices that lead to more freedom and fulfillment.

TheDesireMap.com/
FREEANDCLEAR

Books. Decks. Meditations.
Print. Digital. Audio.

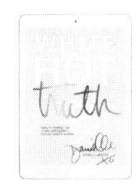

We have a gift for you!
25% OFF
your order!

CODE: WEFRIENDS

DANIELLELAPORTE.COM/
SHOP

ALSO BY DANIELLE . . .

The Desire Map: A Guide to Creating Goals with Soul. The Desire Map Planner Program. *The Fire Starter Sessions: A Soulful + Practical Guide to Creating Success on Your Own Terms. White Hot Truth: Clarity for Keeping It Real on Your Spiritual Path*, #Truthbomb decks, and meditation kits!

We have a gift for you! Go to our shop and use this code to receive 25% off your order. *(Facilitator Programs not included.)*

Photo: Anastasia Chomlack

DANIELLE LAPORTE . . . is a member of Oprah's Super Soul 100, and creator of The Desire Map course and series. The book has been translated into nine languages, a day planner program, and a workshop and coaching program in 15+ countries. She's also the author of *White Hot Truth: Clarity for Keeping It Real on Your Spiritual Path* and *The Fire Starter Sessions*. She was a bartender, apartment manager, nanny, and eventually . . . she ran her own publicity agency and a future-studies think tank studying trends for the Pentagon and the World Bank. Now she writes poetry and speaks about conscious living. She is also a mother to a son.

Named one of the "Top 100 Websites for Women" by *Forbes*, over 5 million people visit **DanielleLaPorte.com** every month for her #Truthbombs. She lives in Vancouver, Canada.

MORE COMMUNE

Leading Teachers, Life-Changing Courses.

Teaching the Teachers
with Marianne Williamson

Redefining Leadership
with Off the Mat, Into the World

Hacking Your Healthcare
with Dr. Mark Hyman

Unwinding Prejudice
with Evelyn Carter

COMMUNE . . . is an online course platform for personal and societal well-being. Our core beliefs:

Practice Old & True: Yoga, meditation, cultivating spirituality, eating locally, composting, cooking mindfully, birthing naturally, dying with dignity, connecting with neighbors and living lightly on the earth. These things are old. These things are true. By rediscovering ideas and practices that are old and true, we can address challenges that are modern and new.

Honor the Teacher: There is no more honourable role than the teacher. Teachers inspire, heal, pass down wisdom, and bring us together. We support their wisdom.

Foster Community: It is easy to see our life's journey as an individual path, separate from others. But the future of the human condition relies on our ability to connect deeply with each other to solve our most salient problems. Out of many, we are one.

COMMUNE
OneCommune.com

IDEAS. DESIRES. WISDOM. . . . spill your desires in every direction

IDEAS. DESIRES. WISDOM. . . . your heart is genius

IDEAS. DESIRES. WISDOM. . . . keep your heart open

IDEAS. DESIRES. WISDOM. . . . do what lights you up

IDEAS. DESIRES. WISDOM. . . . prioritize pleasure

IDEAS. DESIRES. WISDOM. . . . clarity creates simplicity